A Survival Guide for

Restaurant Professionals

A Survival Guide for

Restaurant Professionals

by Alan Gelb and Karen Levine

THOMSON

™

DELMAR LEARNING

Australia Canada Mexico Singapore Spain United Kingdom United States

A Survival Guide for Restaurant Professionals
Alan Gelb and Karen Levine

Vice President, Career Education Strategic Business Unit:
Dawn Gerrain

Director of Editorial:
Sherry Gomoll

Acquisitions Editor:
Matthew Hart

Editorial Assistant:
Lisa Flatley

Director of Production:
Wendy A. Troeger

Production Manager:
Carolyn Miller

Production Editor:
Kathryn B. Kucharek

Director of Marketing:
Wendy Mapstone

Cover Design:
Joe Villanova

© 2005 by Thomson Delmar Learning. Thomson, the Star logo, and Delmar Learning are trademarks used herein under license.

Printed in Canada
1 2 3 4 5 XXX 08 07 06 05 04

For more information contact Thomson Delmar Learning, 5 Maxwell Drive, PO Box 8007, Clifton Park, NY 12065-2919.

Or you can visit our Internet site at http://www.delmarlearning.com.

For permission to use material from this text or product, submit a request online at http://www.thomsonrights.com
Any additional questions about permissions can be submitted by email to thomsonrights@thomson.com

Library of Congress Cataloging-in-Publication Data

Gelb, Alan.
  A survival guide for restaurant professionals / Alan Gelb and Karen Levine.
    p. cm.
  Includes index.
  ISBN 1-4018-4093-0
1. Food service. 2. Restaurants. I. Levine, Karen. II. Title.
  TX911.G43 2004
  647.95 023—dc22

2004045973

NOTICE TO THE READER

Contents

mation

Acknowledgments

We would like to thank the many professionals who took the time to share their thoughts, insights, and reflections. We would particularly like to thank Anthony J. (Toby) Strianese, Chairperson of Hotel, Culinary Arts and Tourism Department, Schenectady County Community College, for all of his expertise and advice. We would also like to thank Lisa Flatley of Thomson Delmar Learning for her help.

Chapter 1

The Whole Enchilada

Few work situations offer as many fascinating dimensions as a restaurant. For those working in the restaurant business, it has it all. First, it is a *business*. As such, it offers the same stimuli and challenges of any business. There are profit margins to keep in mind, marketing strategies to develop, accounting procedures to stay on top of, personnel issues to resolve, and competition to withstand. Those who love business see it as a great game—real-life Monopoly™—with setbacks that may make you lose a turn and triumphs that can thrust you ahead of other players. Restaurants are businesses that can shower cash and cachet on those involved with them, and as businesses they will always be around. After all, people have to eat, don't they?

Restaurants also provide extraordinary work environments in that they create highly intimate worlds where interpersonal relationships are key to success. The restaurant business also, obviously, involves a huge amount of interfacing with the public. Indeed, without that contact, there would be no restaurant business. Dealing with the public's ongoing desire to be surprised and delighted, as well as the fickleness of public taste, is a major challenge in and of itself. In a way, the restaurant business is a bit like the theater. It is a business in the sense that you have to "sell seats," but it is a business where the force of individual personalities plays a large part and where a certain fortitude for gambling is required. Being in the restaurant business is not like manufacturing corrugated cardboard boxes. The highs are much higher, and the lows are much lower. In short, this business in which you've found yourself is a tough and an exhilarating one. So how are you feeling about it? Let's take your temperature and see.

Think about the following questions. If you wish, you can even use this as a real exercise where you jot down your feelings, just for yourself. Perhaps when you finish this book, you'll want to go back to your notes to see whether you feel the same way. Let's start with your energy level. How tired *are* you? Most people who work in the restaurant business will find themselves very, very tired. It is a world of long hours and considerable stress. Did you realize that going into it? Would knowing it have made a difference in your ultimate decision to pursue this path? A little later in this book, you'll find tips on handling fatigue and stress. These problems are difficult ones, but there are many good ways to go about remedying them.

How are you doing with your coworkers? As we've said, a restaurant is an environment where your relationships with people prove to be profoundly important. In some sense, a restaurant is like a family. You spend a great deal of time with a relatively small group of people with whom you share much, including meals. Sometimes that feels wonderful; other times it feels maddening—just like a family. Is one member of this "family"—a "little brother" or an "older sister" perhaps—driving you crazy? Does your manager feel like your father or mother? Are people intruding on your personal space in ways that seem inappropriate? If the answer to any of the above is yes, then don't despair. In chapter 5, you will learn the best way to handle these interrelationships. We offer strategies for conflict resolution, tips on anger management, information on gender bias and cultural diversity, and much more.

There's also the question of how you're pursuing your goals. In fact, do you even *have* goals, or do you sometimes feel as though you're going about your career in a totally off-the-cuff way? Does the thought nag at you that you landed in this field almost accidentally? Are you even sure that you *want* to be in this field? Are you unclear about how to climb the ladder? Do you have a five-year plan? A 10-year plan? Do you dare dream about opening your own restaurant? Your own chain of restaurants? Do you want to see your name on restaurants all over the country . . . all over the globe? John's? Nancy's? Pedro's? Kim's? It could happen, you know. You'll find many insights in this book about how to define and pursue your goals.

Also key to your success in this field is your ability to achieve a high level of organization and to stay on task. You're in a very detail-oriented profession. You may find yourself dealing with scheduling, purchasing, reservations, and other issues where a mistake on your part could prove costly. Chapter 4 includes many useful tips designed to help you excel in the area of organizational skills.

As we've said, restaurant work is hard work. It's like throwing a party every night or, even more, like putting on a show. A restaurant experience, as we all know, is not just about the food, although the food is perhaps the most complex and powerful aspect of the evening. The patron's experience is also about the service, the ambiance, and the special little things that can make the restaurant visit so memorable. All of this takes work, and some of it, particularly if you're waitstaff, is plain, hard, physical work, such as lifting and bending. Wherever you are in the organization, there is the strain of having to meet a relentless and an unforgiving standard of excellence. To fall short of that standard means the likelihood of losing a customer, and we don't have to tell you what that means. So chapters 7 and 8 deal with the issue of stress and how to keep yourself physically at the top of your game.

Other chapters in this book offer tips from those in specific areas. We will be talking to managers, assistant managers, waitstaff, bartenders, maître d's, captains, hosts and hostesses, those in charge of booking reservations, cashiers, purchasers, distributors, wine stewards, banquet sales managers, and owners and supervisors. These people will be speaking anonymously and will pull no punches. They will tell it like it is, and you will come away with insights and information that will prove valuable during your own experience.

Although careers in the restaurant field can be challenging and even difficult in many respects, the excitement and the opportunity are very attractive to newcomers. A recent study conducted by Florida International University's School of Hospitality Management showed that hospitality majors were passionate about their future careers in the industry, saw great potential for advancement, and were, to a large extent, already engaged in on-the-job training as they worked toward their degrees. Additionally, in this study sample, nearly 44 percent of the respondents had already selected hospitality for their future careers by the time they had graduated from high school (*Nation's Restaurant News*, March 24, 2003, p. 16). It's a great field that you've chosen, and your goal is to make the most of it. One way to maximize your experience is to learn from others. That's what this book is all about. The tips and insights you'll hear from those in the field hopefully will inspire you and, in some cases, alert you to pitfalls to be avoided. Let's begin by hearing some of the responses from our restaurant professionals when asked: What's the first thing people should know when they decide to enter this field?

✪ Ever since September 11, 2001, it's been tough being in the field because of all the obvious economic downturns. At the same time, though, I think I've felt more than ever how important restaurants are to people. Restaurants are where people go to propose marriage, to tell their partners that they're pregnant, to meet someone you don't know for the first time who might turn out to be the love of your life. Restaurants are where you go to have a business meeting in a pleasant and vibrant setting, to celebrate an important occasion, to impress visitors from out of town, and just to go and be with friends, or maybe even to just not be by yourself. Restaurants can be a thrill, and restaurants can be a comfort. For me, being involved with restaurants is being involved with a business that gives people enormous pleasure, if you do it right, and that, in and of itself, is very gratifying.

✪ It's very helpful to learn from the ground up. Even if you're right out of an academic program in the hospitality field, there's no substitute for on-site learning. That's exactly why on-site learning, in the form of internships, is built into so many hospitality programs. You want to understand the front of the house, and you want to understand the back of the house. You have to see how the parts fit into each other.

✪ First and foremost, you have to know what you're doing. You're handling some really big-time responsibilities when you work in the restaurant business. There are a lot of ways people can get hurt, not only in accidents, but in serving bad food. People can even die when mistakes are made. I think it's critical to have an awareness of that and to assume responsibility with absolute seriousness of purpose.

❦ The good news is you're never bored. The bad news is you're never bored. No, seriously, I mean it. You're working in a field that's full of a certain kind of drama. You're dealing with food and flowers and creative personalities and performance, performance, performance! The bad news, as I said, is that it's never boring. When no two days are the same, a certain kind of fatigue can hit you where all you're dreaming of is a nice desk job you can leave behind at five o'clock and go home to uninterrupted leisure time. What must *that* be like?

❦ Anyone entering this field should understand how much pressure is involved. You're not dealing with a product that you can leave hanging around in the warehouse until people are ready for it. When you make it, you've got to sell it. You're investing in materials—fine meats, fresh fish, quality produce, cheeses—and if you can't move them, then you "eat" them, if not literally, then in terms of your bottom line.

❦ What I really love about the restaurant business—and this is the nugget I'd want to pass on to others coming into the field—is that you can always do better. You can continually strive upward toward amazing standards of excellence. You can aim for the best food, the best service, the best ambiance, the best operation. It's an incredible lifelong stimulus to be involved in something like that.

❦ A good thing to hear right at the start—even if you find it hard to hear it—is that working as a restaurant professional may involve your making real sacrifices on the quality-of-life front. I mean, it's not like you're a soldier at war or something—you can have a perfectly fine life—but it's probably going to be a different kind of life than your brother-in-law's or your neighbor's or your friend's. You're going to be the one who works on the weekends and works on holidays and works in the evening. You're going to be the one who's probably going to have to miss most of your kid's soccer games and the school play, and as far as New Year's Eve with your spouse—forget about it.

🕭 What's been an education and a challenge for me is that I set my sights very high—I wanted to work in a really great restaurant—and the fact is that I haven't been working in really great restaurants. I've been managing pretty ordinary restaurants, and that can be a little frustrating. But the good news is that I've also been successful in bringing in some excellent innovations into the places I've managed. I started a brunch at one of the places that became very popular, and I was involved in a complete refurbishing of another restaurant I worked in, and that was an education. Hey, it's all an education—just don't set your sights too high.

🕭 The thing that I'd want to telegraph to anyone entering the field is that there is so much opportunity awaiting you. There's no ceiling to what you can do. That's because there's a real entrepreneurial bent running through this field. Oh, sure, you can get a great job managing the restaurants for a hotel chain, and you can work your way up to vice president, and you can have a great career that way. But maybe you'll want to do something like that for a while and then start your own operation. It's all up to you.

The Career "Menu"

Before we go any farther, we want to identify the players on the field and ensure that if you're reading this, you've found yourself with the right book. We are dealing with the full range of restaurant professionals, as differentiated from culinary professionals. In other words, in this book, we're dealing with the "front of the house" instead of the "back of the house." So who exactly are we talking about? Let's have a look.

The Dining Room Brigade

Escoffier, the fabled father of modern cooking, instituted a whole new system of operations for large hotels and restaurants, what he called "the Kitchen Brigade." In this system, everybody had a distinct task, which meant that no one duplicated anyone else's work. This system provided efficiency, safety, and an *esprit de corps*. The members of the kitchen brigade, as designated by Escoffier, included the chef, the *sous-chef*, and the station chefs or cooks. Escoffier also designated a parallel hierarchy for the front of the house, "the Dining Room Brigade." The traditional line of authority in a formal dining room included the following players:

❦ The *maître d'hôtel* or the *dining room manager*. The maître d'hôtel, usually known as the "maître d", is the person who is primarily responsible for running the entire dining room operation. The maître d' trains and supervises all service personnel, oversees the selection of wine, organizes the seating in the dining room, and often collaborates with the chef to design the menu.

❧ The *sommelier* or *chef de vin* is more commonly known on our shores as the *wine steward*. The wine steward is the restaurant professional who assumes primary responsibility for the wine service. This entails purchasing the wine, preparing the wine list, helping guests make wine selections, and serving the wine as it should be served. In the absence of a wine steward, these duties will generally fall to the maître d'.

❧ The *chef de salle* or *head waiter* falls between the maître d' and the captain (discussed next). The head waiter is generally in charge of service for the entire dining room.

❧ The *chef d'etage* is more commonly known as the *captain*. The captain is the restaurant professional who deals most directly with the guests once they have been seated. The captain explains the various items on the menu to the guests, answers their questions, and takes their orders. The captain also prepares any table-side food, such as carving, deboning, or presenting a *flambé*. In the absence of a captain, these duties will be performed by the front waiter (discussed next).

❧ The *chef de rang* is the *front waiter*. The front waiter is the restaurant professional who makes sure that the table is properly set for each course, that the food is delivered to the table as it should be, and that each and every need of each and every guest is duly met.

◖◗ The *demi-chef de rang* or *commis de rang* is the restaurant professional known as the *back waiter*, *busboy*, or *busing person*. This position is usually assigned to the least experienced dining room workers. Duties include clearing plates between courses, filling water glasses, and things of that ilk.

In this book, we gather tips from all of the aforementioned and explore the domains of other restaurant professionals as well, including the purchaser and distributor, whose duties involve overseeing the supplying of provisions for the restaurant, assuring quality control, and determining that inventory is met.

We also talk to other front-of-the-house professionals, including hosts and hostesses, reservations persons, cashiers, and banquet sales managers. From there, we hear from those at the helm: the restaurant and banquet managers. Finally, we check in with restaurant owners to see what they have to say about life at the top.

Regardless of which position you fill as a restaurant professional, certain universal concerns should be kept in mind. As we mentioned earlier, some of these include stress and burnout, conflict with fellow workers, issues of organization and efficiency, and the need to maintain optimal health and energy. The nitty-gritty advice that fills this book—how to take a phone reservation, how to present a check, how to count change— must be put into the context of more sweeping principles by which to start living your life and conducting your career. We have developed these principles during the course of writing books for professionals in any number of vocational fields. The Seven Guiding

Principles that you are about to learn are designed to help you determine what you value most in your life and how you can make room for these things.

The Seven Guiding Principles

Once you've read through the Seven Guiding Principles, you will want to do your best to keep them firmly in your mind. The way you choose to do so is up to you. Maybe you'll remember them best if you keep them in your wallet on a card that you can pull out at quiet moments. Maybe you'd like to paste the card onto the dashboard of your car so you can review them when you're stopped at a traffic light. Maybe you're more of an auditory learner than a visual learner, so you might make a tape in which you state the following principles and then listen to it as you drive, or when you work out on an exercise bike. Or maybe your best bet is to turn these principles into some kind of rhyme or counting song that you can chant at quiet times or, ritually, once a day, in the morning or before you go to sleep at night.

Your goal in internalizing these Seven Guiding Principles is to develop a healthy, "holistic" perspective of your career that will sustain you over the long run. Success is a great thing, but let's not forget that the healthiest goal is for you to enjoy life, have fun doing what you're doing, and be able to remember, at the end of the day, exactly what it is you love about your work and why you chose to go into the field in the first place.

Principle #1: Become an Active Listener

To a large degree, your work depends on listening. You are part of a team, and if you can't hear what others have to say, then your colleagues may wind up feeling neglected, ignored, and angry or disappointed with you, while you may come away feeling isolated and unhappy with yourself. Listening is the key to communication, and communication is one of the truly central behaviors in the human experience. The more we are able to listen—and the better we become at hearing what is said—the more we can expect to get out of our work life and out of life in general.

Later in this book, we discuss listening skills, with tips on specific techniques. But let's start by stressing the importance of taking time out of your busy day to listen to others to really hear what they have to say. Immersing yourself in the demands of the all-involving job of working in a restaurant means that you may have to "filter out" a lot of things, prioritizing what you choose to hear in order to stay afloat. This "filtering out" may seem like self-preservation, but over time it can actually intensify your experience of stress. You may begin to feel very much alone, as though there's an invisible wall separating you from others. You may find that your ability to relieve stress is much improved by keeping open the lines of communication. If you manage to do this, you will benefit from the contact and camaraderie that is there to be mined in your relationships with your colleagues and even your customers. Stay alert, however, to the fact that when we talk about communication, we are really talking about engaging with others in *real* dialogue. We're not talking about "How are you? Fine" and a slap on the back. By real dialogue, we mean saying what you have to say and listening to what others have to say to you.

Principle #2: Think Outside of the Box

In considering Principle #2, first let us define the terms. What do we mean by "the box"? We mean the place that you put yourself into, day in and day out. For some, that place may feel comfortable; for others, it may feel tight and restrictive. Either way, it's still a box, and you're still limiting yourself by remaining within its walls. Maybe the box is the restaurant that you've come to—a place that does not even come close to your dreams and the fantasies that propelled you on this vocational path. Were you dreaming of reflecting pools, a one-of-a-kind tasting menu, and beautiful people lined up at the bar, sipping jewel-colored cocktails as they waited for you, the person with the power, to seat them? Or have you, in reality, found yourself in a chain restaurant, cleaning ketchup off the walls where some unruly youngsters have flung it? The gulf between your fantasy and your reality is just another kind of box that you may have gotten yourself into. Your task, right now, is to get yourself out of that box. How do you do so? Maybe you'll take up a new interest—swimming, let's say, or bird-watching. Something that will let you start to see things in a new way. Maybe you'll take a trip—to New Orleans, to Chicago—somewhere different, where you can gain a fresh perspective. Maybe you'll get together once a month with friends to dine at new restaurants off the beaten path. The idea is to get some *new* ideas, to pull yourself up out of your rut or bring yourself down to earth—whatever is called for. Keep in mind too that continuing education is a reliable prescription for living by this second guiding principle. As long as you're learning, you stand a very good chance of thinking outside of that box.

Principle #3: Take Time to Figure Out What You Find Most Satisfying

Not everyone who becomes a front-of-the-house restaurant professional can actually tell you why he or she chose that path. Back-of-the-house professionals—the chefs, the *sous-chefs*, the pastry chefs, and all—usually can cite a very clear-cut directional path. They always loved food, so they chose to become chefs. But front-of-the-house people usually wind up doing what they are doing for much more diverse reasons. Maybe they come from a "restaurant family," and they're carrying on the tradition. If this is the case, they might feel good about that—traditions are nice, after all—or not so good about that, if they really wanted to become a dancer or a pilot but were pressured to go in the direction their family pointed them. Or maybe they wound up in a front-of-the-house job because after experimenting with the back of the house, they had to admit that they weren't really right for that work. They might not have felt sufficiently creative or even adequately interested in cooking. Having worked in the front of the house, perhaps they discovered that what really raced their motor, what they were really *good* at, was dealing with the public. "I love the interface with the public," one of our professionals told us. "I love when they come in and they look all excited because it's grandma and grandpa's golden anniversary, and knowing that I'm a part of that and that I can make this evening so special for them is enormously gratifying to me." To come to an awareness of what it is you really enjoy and appreciate is to discover one of the Seven Guiding Principles that can really change your life.

In developing our Seven Guiding Principles, we came upon the work of Mihaly Cziksentmihalyi, Ph.D., professor of psychology at the Drucker School of Management at Clermont Graduate University. In a groundbreaking study conducted with a group of adolescents, his findings are relevant to this discussion. The adolescents in Dr. Cziksentmihalyi's study were outfitted with beepers that went off eight times a day over the course of one week each year. Every time the beepers signaled, the adolescents would report to

Dr. Cziksentmihalyi what they were doing and how they were feeling about it. Among other things, Dr. Cziksentmihalyi discovered that when his subjects were involved in activities they enjoyed, they were able to develop a sense of what he called "flow," that great feeling of energy that makes people want to continue doing what they're doing and return to it whenever possible.

In our next chapter, we offer a tool and a technique by which you can begin to figure out the activities that give you the greatest sense of flow. You'll learn how to keep track of the way you spend your time, and you will be able to assess how you really feel about what you're doing. We'll take you through your day in detail—before, after, and during work—and we'll show you how to make a meaningful analysis that will reveal those activities that leave you feeling the most satisfied and those that leave you feeling the least fulfilled. This kind of honest assessment represents a critical step before you move on to Principle #4.

Principle #4: Create Time for the Things You Care About

As a restaurant professional, you probably work long and erratic hours. As we said earlier, you may be tired a great deal of the time. Do you ever find yourself stepping off of the treadmill of your life and asking yourself, "Is that all there is?" If this is a common refrain that plays in the back of your mind, then it's time to gain control of your life by "recharging." Maybe you'll have to start shifting things around, collaborating with other people, including those in your private life, to enable you to have somewhat more flexibility so that you can alleviate that treadmill feeling. Don't shake your head and say "Impossible." Anything's possible, and too many of us carry around a "can't do" attitude, when the fact is, we "*can* do." We *can* make changes in our lives, even if they're small and subtle ones, which can affect you in powerful ways over time.

Which kinds of changes are we talking about? Okay, let's imagine that you're feeling chronically fatigued, achy throughout your body, and generally blah. A friend whose judgment you value tells you that what you really need to do is take up yoga—30 minutes a day. Thirty minutes a day? Impossible! But hold on a moment. Maybe you can make some changes in your routine that will allow you to get what you need. Maybe the change will be as simple as getting up a half hour earlier in the morning and doing yoga at a time when you can expect not to be interrupted. If you live with someone, and your partner has some flexibility, then maybe you'll be able to trade jobs and chores. Maybe your partner can walk the dog, feed the baby, water the plants, or whatever while you do what you need to do for yourself. Then you can make up for it on the other end of the day. The point is that you really owe it to yourself to make the effort, because when you can best meet your own needs, you stand a better chance of meeting the needs of others.

Principle #5: *Learn to Enjoy What's in Front of You*

One of the core ideas of Buddhism is "mindfulness." To be mindful means to live in the moment, and learning to live in the moment is enormously beneficial to those of us trying to clear away the clutter in our lives. Those who practice mindfulness learn how to focus on what is beautiful in the here and now, not what is worrisome in the future or the past. As a restaurant professional, you may very well have too much on your plate. You may be supervising a team of individuals, each of whom comes to you with his or her complaints and grievances. You may be dealing with a variety of outside vendors and suppliers difficult to keep on top of. Or you may be trying—sometimes unsuccessfully—to decode the desires and demands of your boss. All or any of these things can lead you to continually be in another place rather than the place you occupy in real space and time.

Think about it. Do you find yourself driving along, worrying about the lobster shipment that is due in, or the private party that threatens to turn rowdy? Do you even realize that there is a beautiful sunset going on right beyond your windshield, or that there's a rainbow in the sky? Stepping back to be mindful—to simply note, experience, and enjoy what is going on in the here and now rather than obsessing about what could have been or might be—is a truly revolutionary way to live. Indeed, no matter how much you actually enjoy your work and appreciate the life you've made for yourself, sometimes it is difficult to resist the pull of the routines in which we are all involved. Sometimes it is nearly impossible to resist the petty disappointments and frustrations that follow us through the day. The practice of mindfulness provides an extraordinary means by which to get ourselves "back into shape." Setting a table doesn't have to be a bore. It can be a time when you appreciate the crispness of the white linen, the gleam of the wine glass, and the competence you bring to your task. Unpacking a crate of fruit doesn't have to be a burdensome chore. It can be a time when you look at the beauty of a pear or an apple, or when you inhale the scent of a ripe peach. Your mindful openness to a real, sensual appreciation of the things you do can help enormously in restoring your appetite for life and for enjoying your work.

Principle #6: Learn to Be Flexible

What's a day without a crisis? Certainly nothing you've ever encountered, we'd wager. Crises are par for the course in the restaurant business. Often there are outsized personalities in the kitchen who enjoy a good blowout, customers who behave like boors, or food shipments that go awry. Your responses when things go wrong will say a lot about your ability to sustain yourself in this career over the long run. Are you the sort to pull out your hair, gnash your teeth, scream at your underlings, or hit the cooking sherry? Or do you inflict punishment on yourself rather than on others, surrendering to migraines, acid reflux, or a variety of other ills? If you find yourself frequently on either of these paths, then this is an excellent time to take stock and make some changes. You can't go on living that way—it's as simple as that.

Let's imagine that you're a highly disciplined person and always do what you set out to do. You like to think of yourself as a well-honed machine that gets the job done. You'll work the longest hours, expend the most energy, and kick into overdrive when the crises hit and the going gets tough. Okay, that's a perfectly reasonable model for your professional conduct, if that's what you choose. But don't forget the other aspects of the picture. You wouldn't drive a machine into the ground, would you? You would take care of it. You would clean it, replace any broken parts, and keep it well oiled and lubricated so its gears wouldn't grind against each other and wear down. So if you enjoy thinking of yourself as a machine—a super-sophisticated machine that can do anything asked of it—then we urge you to think of flexibility as the lubricant that will preserve your working parts. Flexibility is your very best weapon against stress, and it will soften the sharp edges that can often factor into your interactions with others. If you sometimes feel like a rubber band ready to snap or a frayed old piece of elastic that can no longer keep up your pajamas, then remember that flexibility is what will keep the rubber supple and the elastic firm and pliable. Like mindfulness, flexibility is a power that is totally available to you and that can be developed and strengthened the more it is practiced.

Principle #7: Prioritize

Having digested six of the Seven Guiding Principles, you can now consider the last—prioritizing. The other principles hopefully have enabled you to focus on what you like to do and how to handle the things you have to do. Now you want to be able to arrange things so some of the tasks that really drag you down can be minimized and some of the activities that boost your feelings of well-being can be maximized. When you start keeping track of your time, as we will show you how to do in the next chapter, it can come as a great surprise to see how much actual choice you have in deciding where to devote your efforts. The way to begin to prioritize is to start asking yourself key questions such as the following:

✐ *What do I need to do to take care of myself that absolutely no one else can do for me?* The answer is totally yours to come up with. It may be a hobby. It may be watching baseball. It may be soaking in a hot tub at the end of a long day. It may be sleeping late once a week. It may be going out to other restaurants to stay fresh and on top of the curve. The answers—and the questions—are yours.

✐ *Which of my responsibilities can be put off for the moment so that I can deal with them later, with no harm done?* This can be a tough one. You'll have to examine your systems to see where there is any give. What about meetings? Can you fold one meeting into another and thereby come up with a little extra free time? Is there something you do every day that you might be able to get away with doing every other day?

📖 *What am I doing that someone else could be doing for me?* Quite a few things, no doubt. Our society is so based on a fundamental tenet of individualism that many of us can't even see the ways in which we can collaborate and delegate. For instance, are you using an assistant or an intern to capacity? By doing so, you will be improving the experience of that other person and at the same time helping yourself. Can you trade off tasks with a coworker? Is one of your coworkers better at something that is a struggle for you, and vice versa? Can you switch without compromising either of your positions?

These questions should be kept in the front of your mind, and you should return to them frequently. Getting into the habit of asking yourself questions such as these also gets you into the habit of thinking differently and finding the ability to prioritize and make your work life more satisfying.

So there we have the Seven Guiding Principles. Think about them, look them over carefully, and return to them as needed but don't expect to embody them and live by them overnight. It doesn't happen that way. Some people may take months or even years to internalize the lessons of these principles. Even then, most have to be vigilant about not letting old and counterproductive habits creep back into control. As time goes on, the more you practice living by these principles, the more they will become second nature. And the more that happens, the more you will be able to appreciate and enjoy a quality of life that you may not have been able to achieve otherwise.

Chapter Reference

Cziksentmihalyi, M. (1991). *The psychology of optimal experience*. New York: HarperCollins.

Chapter 2

Taking Inventory

*a*s a restaurant professional, you fully understand the importance of inventory. If you don't have enough potatoes, cutlery, waitstaff, cinnamon, detergent . . . well, you're going to be in trouble. The recommended procedure for many restaurant managers is to take some form of inventory every day and then utilize other, more wide-ranging inventories on a weekly, monthly, semi-annual, and annual basis. This prevents them from running out of what they need. With good planning, this shouldn't happen. Running out of steam on a personal basis is also a bad idea, and to protect your energy, your commitment, and your sense of satisfaction with your work, we will teach you some simple ways to keep track of how you spend your time. You'll also learn how to assess what you're getting out of the time you devote to your work and to your other interests.

In the restaurant business, there is not a great deal of time for reflection . . . as long as business is good. The ongoing pressure to get through one shift and on to the next means that most of us try our best just to get through the day. When people ask, "How are you doing?," we generally answer, "Fine." We may not feel "fine," but nobody wants to hear otherwise, and we don't want to go into it anyway. There simply isn't time. But in that tired exchange, something very real and valuable can get lost. The details of our day become blurred, and we run the risk of becoming just as disinterested in or inattentive to what is going on in our lives as the people who keep asking us that same hollow question. Our honesty, self-awareness, and empathy dwindle, and we become mechanical beings, going through the paces.

One of the most important messages that we hope to convey in this book is that every day of your life *is* special and deserves to be treated that way. To that end, we suggest that you carefully consider how you spend your time by keeping a record of your activities. Most of us spend at least 16 out of every 24 hours a day awake and, to some degree, active. For many of us, those 16 hours can stretch out to 17, 18, or even 19 hours. During that time, much of what we do makes us feel good—or at least that's the hope. We are kept busy with activities that engage us intellectually, emotionally, physically, or spiritually. We may even be lucky enough to feel energized and happy as a result of the work we do. When that happens, we experience the sense of "flow" discussed in the previous chapter. Unfortunately, however, many of us spend a good part of our time doing activities and tasks that offer no flow whatsoever. We're left bored, restless, frustrated, and anxious. We start asking ourselves questions such as, "What's it all about, anyway?"

As a restaurant professional, you understand exactly what we're talking about, don't you? When you find yourself dealing with boorish customers who treat you like dirt or temperamental coworkers who carry on like divas, it's not easy to "feel the flow." The demands of day-to-day living also can sap you of that precious flow. Tasks such as paying bills, doing the laundry, going grocery shopping, commuting, and chauffeuring the children around do not fill one with wonder. In fact, when these tasks feel unending, as they so often do, we can be brought down to a dispirited place, and it will take much effort to bring us up again. Hopefully, we can all step back a little and convince ourselves that we have more control over our lives than we sometimes feel we do. When we really start to think about how we use our time and how we *feel* about how we use our time, then we can begin to make the necessary changes and adjustments in our schedules that will make us feel better about what we're doing.

The goal in writing this book is to help you find the right ways to focus on your life. The kind of intense attention that we are advocating can ultimately help you simplify what you're doing and make your life and your work more satisfying. To that end, we're going to ask you to do something that a lot of people won't find easy. We want you to look at how you spend your time—the precious minutes and hours of your day—not just at work, but also before you leave for work and when you get home. In so doing, it is our belief that you will come to see how your different emotional spheres interface.

In thinking over our conversations with the many restaurant professionals we spoke with in connection with this book, we are reminded of a woman, Phyllis, who worked as a banquet sales manager for a hotel in Fort Worth, Texas. Phyllis came to the restaurant profession after having been a manager of a retail clothing store that went belly up. She had pounded the pavement for some months before finding an opportunity that looked like it might pay her something close to what she had been making. She talked herself into the job, even without any experience in the area of banquet sales, and she was determined to make good. And make good she did, for she was a quick study and a relentlessly hard worker. She was so relentless, in fact, that when she had a day off, she generally did not have a clue as to how to relax and enjoy herself. Usually she brought work home with her. After about eight or nine months of being stuck in this syndrome, her sister, Jocelyn, visited from Denver. "Phyllis," she asked, after having been with her for a few days, "where are your friends?"

Jocelyn's question was a wake-up call for Phyllis. Although making and keeping friends had always been important to her, she had let that part of herself lapse during this recent phase of her life, and the realization that she had done so was painful. However, being the hard worker that she was, she set about to remedy the situation. She recognized that it was time to develop an interest totally outside of her work, and that this interest should be one that would put her in contact with people outside of the restaurant profession. One thing that Phyllis had always been clear about was that she loved nature, so she joined a chapter of the Appalachian Club. Whenever she had free time, she would seek out some activity sponsored by the club. Maybe it would be a hike, a lecture, or an environmental project. Whatever it was, she joined in, and before she knew it, she had met a whole group of people who shared common interests and represented a welcome relief from her pressured work situation.

Phyllis's story is hardly a one-of-a-kind tale. So many of us become so single-minded in our quest to achieve our goals that we allow our relationships, our physical well-being, and our enjoyment of life to fall by the wayside. We mustn't let that happen. For Phyllis, a walk in the woods was incredibly restorative. For you, it could be taking a class in photography, ballroom dancing, throwing a pot (in a pottery class, not out of anger!), taking up golf, or who knows what. Maybe you just need some vegging-out time in front of the TV, with a pint of ice cream and a good video. Whatever it is you need, hopefully this chapter will teach you how to monitor yourself so you can learn to fulfill your needs as they present themselves.

Keeping Track

As we have said, a lot gets lost in the shuffle of a normal busy day. Sometimes the day is so hectic you forget to eat or even go to the bathroom. Given that, the more subtle aspects of the day (Were you satisfied with your performance? Did you learn anything? Did you have meaningful interactions with other people?) can easily be obscured. Therefore, in order for you to develop a real awareness of how you spend your day—and in order to keep track of how you *feel* about the way you spend your day—we suggest that you undertake the following assignment. Better yet, why don't you think of this section as a kind of workbook? So grab a pencil and paper, and roll up your sleeves and get to work. We'll begin by taking a look at the sections that follow. The headings include:

- Start/Stop/Total
- Activity
- Feelings
- Efficiency
- What's My Role?
- End-of-Day Analysis

Copy these headings into a notebook, one that is small enough to carry around comfortably throughout the day. A little, spiral-bound memo pad that can be tucked into your pocket would be ideal. In this notebook, you will be recording—you also can think of it as logging, if you're of a nautical bent— exactly what you do with your time during any given day.

We understand that there will be times when you will undoubtedly find this exercise just another distraction from your busy schedule. We're sorry to be making these demands on you, but putting in some extra time now on these exercises will free up your time down the line. This method works especially well if you keep at it for an entire week, or even beyond. Doing so allows you to examine the pattern of your weekends which, for many restaurant professionals, are particularly intense.

We recognize that some days it may be difficult and in some cases nearly impossible for you to find the few moments necessary to log your activities. When you're in the middle of carving a roast or serving a Baked Alaska or running a meeting with your staff, it may not feel like the right time to whip out your little notebook and start making notes. Certainly the point of these exercises, and this book as a whole, is to make your life easier, not more difficult, so just do your best. Whenever you come up for air, jot down what you can. Use whichever shorthand methods make sense for you. If possible, try to glance at your watch so you can make a mental note of the time you begin and end an activity. The actual jotting-down part can always come later.

If that's all clear, then let's begin, shall we?

Start/Stop/Total

It is time to take a good, long look at your day. What kind of day was it? Did you stop a fight between two difficult employees? Did you figure out a way to save money? Did you come up with a winning, creative idea for how to promote your restaurant during the off-season? Did any or all of that feel good? Sure it did. But how about the stuff that didn't feel so good? How about the fact that you missed your kid's soccer game or had to read the riot act to someone who came to work dressed inappropriately or had to deal with your boss's whim that made no sense to you whatsoever?

Well, some days are like that, filled with good and bad things. Sometimes a few bad things in a row wipe out anything good that happens. That's why it's so important to get into the habit of paying attention to your day. Keeping a journal will help you establish that habit.

As we've said, in order for you to take stock of your day, you're going to have to be conscious of the clock. That means from the moment your alarm goes off in the morning until you close your eyes at night, *you are paying attention to what you're doing.* An extraordinary idea, no? Think about the many things you do in the course of a day and how much of it you take for granted: getting dressed; taking care of your houseplants and your cat; paying bills; reviewing the day's deliveries from the vendors; attending to advertising and promotion; checking the books; following around the inspector from the Board of Health . . . the list goes on.

Each time you begin a new activity, make a note of the "start" time. Do the same when you finish that activity, writing down the "stop" time before you move on to your next activity. And don't forget—*everything* you do during the day should be noted. Closing your eyes for five minutes? Write it down. Getting a cup of coffee? Write it down. Catching your breath? Down it goes. Eventually you will be asked to tally the "total time spent," but you can do that later. For now, in the middle of a crazy day, don't burden yourself further by adding, subtracting, or performing any other feats of higher math. What we want you to do is just make notes with simple, straight numbers of whatever it is you do—30 minutes of yoga; 25 minutes to drive to work; 15 minutes to sample the new wine delivery; 6 minutes to sweep up a broken dish; and so on—and then tally the numbers at the end of the day.

Is all of this worth the trouble? Let's hear from the following restaurant professionals who have "gotten with the program":

◖◗ I had a love/hate relationship with the **Start/Stop/Total** exercise. In the beginning, it was a real drag to have to devote that amount of energy and attention to how I spent my time. But then, the more I did it, the better I started to feel about myself. I had this record—on a page, in black and white—and I started to feel, like, hey, you know what? You manage to get a heck of a lot done in 24 hours, buddy. Good for you!

◖◗ This is not the easiest thing to do in the beginning, but I've got to tell you—it's really worth the effort. You discover yourself doing things that when you realize how much time they're taking your jaw drops. It's like these patterns that you can only see if you look very carefully. For instance, I've got a pretty high-pressure job—I'm an assistant manager in a very popular restaurant outside of Boston—and I don't have a lot of free time to myself. My sister, on the other hand, is a stay-at-home mom with a two-year-old. She'll think nothing of calling me at work twice a day and telling me every little drama that's going on in her life. Now I love my sister to pieces, but when I started doing the **Start/Stop/Total** exercise, it hit me just how much time I was spending talking to Annie in the course of any given day. I had to sit her down and say, "I can't do this, babe. You can call me in the evening, but don't call me during the day unless it's an emergency." I think she was a little hurt at first, but she survived.

📢 The thing that I liked about this exercise is that it shows you these patterns, and then you can begin to make changes because the inefficiency of what you're doing is staring you in the face. For instance, exercise is important to me, and I've been trying to factor in a run three or four days a week. Two days a week, I have to drive my daughter to a violin lesson a half hour from my house, and I sit there, in the car, waiting for her. I discovered a track at the high school near her music teacher's house and now, while she's having her lesson, I'm getting my run in. Of course, she's mortified when I show up all hot and sweaty, but hey—that's life. The point is that I don't know if I would have made the connection if I hadn't done the **Start/Stop/Total** assignment.

Activity

The next part of the workbook assignment is to fill in your **Activity** chart. For most people, this is a real eye-opener. You won't believe how many hats you wear in a single day. There you are as a manager (discuss tardiness with Diane), as a public representative of your restaurant (do radio spot on menu ideas for Thanksgiving), as a spouse or romantic partner (take Kim to the Palace for anniversary dinner), as a friend (going-away party for Max), as a son or daughter (take Mom for her checkup), as a parent (take Lily to the dentist), as neighbor, as a Boy Scout leader, as a church deacon, as a home owner, and much, much more. Your **Activity** entries will help give you the "big picture" on all of this. The more specific you are when making your entries, the more information and insight you'll have at the end of the exercise.

As you're keeping track of all of this, keep in mind that everything you write down is for your eyes only. No one else is participating in this exercise, and no one else will read what you write, unless, that is, you choose to share it. Your goal here is to learn more about yourself—how you use your time and how you *feel* about how you use your time. Let's hear what it was like for our restaurant professionals to work on this task:

📻 Making up the **Activity** chart was pretty interesting. For one thing, it showed me how much I actually get done in one day. I'm a Superwoman! No, seriously, I obviously have been aware all along that I get a lot done, but seeing it there, in black and white, was reassuring in a way. I can juggle work and family and taking care of my own needs really well. I guess that comes with experience and maturity.

From doing the **Activity** chart, I realized that, in any given day, there's so much donkey work I have to do. I'm a purchaser for a restaurant in Cincinnati, and if you asked me whether I like my work or not, I would have said it's fine. But after having done the **Activity** chart, I'm not sure how fine it really is. I might want to reorganize my life so that I'm doing something more flexible and entrepreneurial, like restaurant consulting maybe. We'll see.

Feelings

Once you've finished an activity, the ideal next move is to jot down your feelings about it as close to the time of the activity as you can. The sooner you jot down these feelings, the more honest your notations will be, and the less likely you are to edit them, either consciously or unconsciously. By no means should you feel that you have to write down long, detailed notes. Any kind of notation that makes sense to you is all that is called for. Maybe it will help if you think in terms of "feeling" words—are you feeling happy, sad, angry, bored, or worried? Another way to approach this is to try seeing where you fall on the spectrum when you think of opposite feelings: are you leaning more toward happy or sad, relaxed or tense, worried or optimistic, loving or angry, energetic or tired, or interested or bored?

What you are trying to do when filling out the **Feelings** section is to gauge the amount of satisfaction you're getting out of your various activities. Obviously not everything we do is designed to bring us joy and pleasure. Getting your car serviced is not going to be an ecstatic experience. Making your bed is not going to transport you (unless you're one of those hospital corners freaks). But seriously, even burdensome tasks may bring some measure of satisfaction if we get to cross them off our list and feel organized and in control. Or, if you're good at doing two things at once, then maybe you can neutralize the boring or irritating aspects of some jobs. Maybe you can listen to opera while you pay bills, or talk to a friend on the phone while you shine your shoes. Keeping a log of the various feelings you experience during the day will help you identify the things that give you pleasure compared to the things that don't. If you see certain patterns emerging—for instance, if music makes a task go easier for you or if you prefer the activities of a team environment rather than individual activities—then you'll have discovered something important about yourself.

Try not to play out all of the angles of your reactions before you actually write them down. The response that comes straight from your gut probably is the most valid one you can have. Again, what you write down is for your eyes only, so don't feel that you have to censor any negative feelings because "somebody might see." This is what one of your colleagues thought abut this part of the activity:

🕮 This was my favorite part of the entire activity. I just thought it was really interesting to examine the feelings I have around all of my activities. Sometimes they're pretty complex. For instance, as waitstaff, I'm involved in setting up tables. On the one hand, that can be boring, but I also enjoy thinking about ways that I can bring an extra bit of creativity to the task. I've always been kind of artistically oriented, so I learned a really pretty way to fold napkins during a trip I made to France. My manager was open to the change, and now we always fold napkins that way. So every time I set the table, I feel good about the contribution I've made. It's a small thing, I know, but I still get satisfaction out of it.

Efficiency

As a restaurant professional, you don't need us to tell you how important it is to be efficient. Bungled reservations, lost orders, inventory mistakes . . . these all add up very quickly and very problematically. Every minute counts in this field. Every minute that a customer is kept waiting is a strike against you, and if too many minutes accumulate, then you run the very real risk of losing that customer forever. So you, as a restaurant professional, are bound to have a particular sensitivity to matters of efficiency . . . or at least you should.

Where are you on the efficiency spectrum? Are you a control freak who doesn't ever want to be crossed, or are you more of a go-with-the-flow sort? As you consider the subject of your efficiency, keep in mind that in some situations, efficiency does not necessarily win you brownie points. For instance, you might have your morning routine down to a science, and everyone in your family is moved out of the house like aluminum cans on a conveyor belt, but it might be a whole lot nicer for everyone and better for your family in the long run if you're less insistent on efficiency and more attuned to the emotional needs of your loved ones. Of course, once again, you are the judge here, and what you write is for your eyes only. If you determine that efficiency does not apply to a particular task, simply write "N/A" (not applicable) in your log. Otherwise, make an effort to rate your efficiency on a 1 to 5 scale for any given activity. This activity was particularly illuminating for some of your colleagues:

🔊 After keeping the log, I saw how inefficient I was in some areas of my life. For instance, I'm always late paying bills, which is ridiculous because I have the money to pay them, thank goodness, but I just get hung up on stuff, and I tend to let my bookkeeping lapse. So after going through this **Efficiency** exercise, I saw, in black and white, how inefficient I was around that, and I've decided to do a lot more automated banking.

🔊 This was pretty eye-opening for me. After doing it, my partner and I sat down to see how we could do better with a lot of the household tasks. Division of labor—that's our new goal.

What's My Role?

Earlier in this chapter, we made the point that all of us, over the course of 24 hours, play a variety of roles. We're managers, wine stewards, maître d's, banquet sales managers, and so on, but we're also husbands, wives, partners, parents, brothers, sisters, sons, daughters, friends, teammates, teachers, coaches, bird-watchers, dog walkers, photographers, needle-pointers . . . you name it. Think about which of these roles you like best. For instance, as a wine steward, do you enjoy educating your customers about wine? Do you enjoy learning about wine from the sales representatives you meet with? As a purchaser, do you appreciate the collaborative role you play on the restaurant team? As a manager, do you enjoy the hiring aspect of your job?

Think about the roles you play, and then, during a given week, compile a list of these roles somewhere in the back of your notebook or pad. As you fill in your log, figure out which roles you've been playing for which activity, but don't feel that you have to record these close to the time of the activity. This category and the next—**End-of-Day Analysis**—can be filled in when you find some quiet time.

End-of-Day Analysis

Now for the big wrap-up. The very last thing you do each day, just before you turn out the lights, is analyze your log. This is your opportunity to really learn something about yourself, and the results can be genuinely surprising. Follow these steps:

1. Begin by totaling the first column, **Start/Stop/Total**. Add up the total for each activity, and note it.

2. Review what you've written in the **Activity** column, and read across the row to **What's My Role?** Think about what your role has been in each activity, and note it in the appropriate place.

	ACTIVITY #1	ACTIVITY #2	ACTIVITY #3
Start Stop Total			
Feelings			
Efficiency			
What's my Role?			

3. When you've filled in the entire **What's My Role?** column, check back to the **Feelings** column and think about which roles you found most pleasurable or satisfying. Note as well

those activities you found least pleasurable or satisfying. Give yourself time to think about how you might rearrange your life to maximize time spent in the pleasurable roles and minimize time spent in those roles you do not enjoy.

4. Look back at your **Start/Stop/Total** column, and match it with the **Feelings** column. How much time did you spend doing things that offered you little satisfaction? How much time did you spend doing the things you most love to do?

5. Think about what was most surprising in your log, and make a note of it. Perhaps it was how much time you spent doing things that you genuinely do not enjoy. Or, maybe—hopefully—it was the other way around. Maybe you're surprised by how much pleasure you took in the more scientific aspects of your work—the mathematical calculations, for instance. Maybe you were surprised by how interested you were in the marketing and public relations aspects of your work as a manager.

6. Repeat this process every day for a week, each day with a new log. At the end of the week, go over all of your notes, paying special attention to the **End-of-the-Day Analysis.** Give yourself ample time to think about what you are reading.

Again, the goal here is to reflect. Ultimately you want to find enough time in your life to do more of what you love and less of what you don't. To achieve that goal, you need to keep track of the following **Seven Guiding Principles,** discussed in Chapter 1.

1. Become an active listener.
2. Think outside of the box.
3. Take time to figure out what you find most satisfying.
4. Create time for the things you care about.
5. Learn to enjoy what's in front of you.
6. Learn to be flexible.
7. Prioritize.

Keeping a log and being mindful of the Seven Guiding Principles is only one step toward making the most of your life as a restaurant professional. The next chapter will introduce you to the very important issue of setting goals for yourself and turning those goals into achievements.

Chapter 3

The Goal Zone

*a*s we stated in an earlier chapter, quite a few of the restaurant professionals to whom we spoke were surprised to find themselves following this path. They may have initially entered a hospitality or culinary program thinking that they wanted to be a chef or the manager of some glamorous hotel, but in time they discovered that their real interest was in the front of the house. The "business" of the restaurant business proved the great attraction for them, or perhaps they came to realize that they had a real affinity for people and enjoyed dealing with the public, or maybe they wound up reorienting because they came to see that cooking was not the right choice for them.

Now that they're committed restaurant professionals, however, they felt that it was time for that element of surprise to take a back seat. Few professionals, after all, want to leave their careers to chance. Although they may have gotten to the front of the house through the back door, now that they feel that they're where they're supposed to be, they wish to continue on their path in ways that make the most of any and all opportunities. After all, they want to be successful, as most people do.

Keep in mind that the definitions of success vary from person to person, and the signs of success vary from profession to profession. In very stable, structured professions, the signs of success are appropriately stable and structured. If you're a teacher in a high school, for instance, you will be up for a tenure review after teaching the required number of years. Your district will determine whether your performance has merited the extraordinary job protection that comes with tenure, and you'll either get it or you won't. Being granted tenure is a highly tangible sign of success. As a restaurant professional, you will never enjoy that particular sign. Restaurant professionals are never "granted tenure." You will never have absolute job protection. Indeed, as a restaurant professional, your job will be particularly vulnerable to changes in the economy. Obviously in a bad economy, people eat out less— that's one of the stark realities of the profession you've chosen. By the same token, in a good economy, people eat out a lot. Why? Because it's fun to eat out. Pretty much everybody *wants* to eat out, so at least you can tell yourself that you're in a field where if you have something good to sell and people have the money to buy it, chances are, things will work out for the best.

Before we go any farther with our discussion of goals, however, we want to devote a bit of time to discussing success, for the two go hand in hand. For most people, goals are the signposts on their way to success. Therefore, it's important to be able to recognize success so you'll know when you get there.

The Fundamentals of Success

Nothing is more public and more personal at the same time than success. What do we mean by this? Well, there is the public "face" of success—the cars, the clothes, the awards, the beautiful man or woman on your arm, the honorary degrees, the testimonial dinners—and these are very important to many of us. Then there is the private reality of success. How do we feel *inside*? Many people who enjoy enormous public success suffer from extreme feelings of inadequacy and shame. Think of Marilyn Monroe, Elvis Presley, Daryl Strawberry—men and women at the pinnacle of their professions who engaged in terribly self-destructive behaviors. In most cases like these, such behaviors emanated from a deeply rooted feeling of inadequacy that public success could never really touch. By the same token, consider the many men and women who lead what appear to be relatively undistinguished lives, with limited resources and lots of career disappointment, but who are still able to draw upon their own profound feelings of self-worth. This feeling of self-worth might be derived from their rewarding family experiences, relationships with friends, work in the community, or rich spiritual or creative life. Wherever it comes from, it enables them to feel like *successful* human beings . . . which obviously they are.

One valuable thing to keep in mind is no matter what our definition of success may be, no one leads a life of absolute success. No one has it all. Movie stars, millionaires, sports figures, and others of that ilk who appear to have it all can suffer from private demons and disappointments, just like the rest of us. They may experience marital strife, health issues, or problems with their offspring. They may commit ethical mistakes or suffer an embarrassing failure after a string of glittering hits. No one goes through life escaping disappointment, so whatever we call "success" has to be considered with that as a given.

We spoke to restaurant professionals about what constituted success for them. Their responses follow:

✎ I think the most important point that I can make when asked about what defines success is that it's a definition that's bound to change—a lot—throughout your life. When I was a kid, right out of school, success for me meant money. Why? Because I didn't have any, my parents didn't have any, and I wanted it. I was lucky enough to make money, and that *was* very important for me, but then the definition of success took on other facets. Then I wanted money plus security. Then I wanted money plus security plus a satisfying relationship with another human being. Then I wanted all of that plus I didn't want to have to work as hard as I had been. The definition keeps changing, because *you* keep changing, and that's exactly as it should be. Sometimes I meet people who at the age of 50 still seem to be operating by the same rules and standards they were using when they were 25, and I think to myself, "You haven't grown much, buddy, have you?"

We live in a society and work in a profession that defines success by how much money you make. I don't think most people would argue with that. But when you start looking around, can you really endorse that definition? What about the rich guy who gets drunk and kills a kid on a bike? That's a success? What about the movie star who's married six times and checks into rehab every three months? That's a success?

When you work in a business, it's virtually impossible not to equate a profitable bottom line with success. If you're making the bucks, then you're successful. I see so many people who get caught up in that and just live these incredibly superficial lives, running after designer bags and designer cars and drinking designer water. Don't get me wrong—I want nice things too, and I've set the bar high for myself. But my real role model is my father. Dad owned a little diner in Waterbury, Connecticut, and he never made a lot of money, but he always served good food, and he always made us feel good. He was successful enough for anybody. He still represents the bottom line for me.

🔊 I can't complain—this field has treated me great. I own two restaurants in San Diego, and I'm living better than I ever thought I would. But the real revelation is that my success hasn't just been about watching my bank account grow . . . although that's been nice, I'm not knocking it. The real revelation is that a big part of my success has been the amount of fun I have doing what I do. Oh, sure, it's exhausting, and sure, there's tons of pressure and late nights and all that, but the overriding feeling I live with is that I'm playing this great game. I get to use my brains and my guts and my heart. I have to watch out not to step on the bad squares, and I have to keep an eye out for who's coming up on my left. I have to remind myself too that even though it's a great game, I'm not using play money. But that's where the real success has been for me—in loving what I do as much I do.

🔊 It's really easy to feel successful when everything's going your way. The challenge is in holding on to those feelings of self-esteem when everything's going wrong. And that'll happen—don't kid yourself. To me, the real measure of success is in how well you survive the tough times. Think of those men and women who made up what we now call "the greatest generation." They survived the depression. They survived World War II. Did better than survive, in fact. They made a whole new world. They were the most successful generation, because they were so strong and resourceful. That's how I want to be remembered—for being successful because I could tough things out when I needed to.

🕭 Some people take success so seriously, and I just want to say, lighten up a little. Sure, it's great to be successful, but it's also great to be able to laugh at yourself when you do a belly flop or slip on a banana peel. What's the problem? It only shows that we're human.

🕭 When I graduated from high school, five different people gave me this book called "The Secrets of Highly Successful People." It was full of good advice, but the one thing that struck me the most was that successful people really know how to see the big picture. The whole enchilada, as it were. Successful people don't get hung up in little niggling details. They know what they want, and they go after it.

🕭 There are a lot of great quotes about success. My favorite comes from Mark Twain. He said success is one-tenth inspiration and nine-tenths perspiration. That is so true, and so wonderfully stated.

🕭 As a young person, I was a really gifted ballerina. All I wanted was to dance with a major ballet company, and my teachers told me I might be good enough. Then when I was 12, I was in an automobile accident, and I never danced again. I had to come up with a whole new definition of who I was and a whole new idea of what success was. Over the next few years, I went to work for my aunt, who owned a restaurant. I liked the people, I liked the work, I liked the whole thing. I put all my energies and focus into the restaurant business, and in time I became my aunt's partner. I think all that ability to focus that I learned as a child with ballet made the difference for me. Whatever I wanted—whatever I came to feel was that thing I could call "success"—I felt I could go after it.

Success Do's and Don'ts

If we can agree that most people want to be successful rather than unsuccessful, then why does it seem so hard for a lot of us? There may be any number of answers to that question. Part of being successful has to do with identifying your talents and resources and applying them where they belong. If you're five feet tall, it probably doesn't make a whole lot of sense to try to be a supermodel or a professional basketball player. If you're tone deaf, it is doubtful that you'll become an opera singer. If you have a physical problem that makes it difficult for you to be on your feet for long hours, you'd probably be better off getting a desk job than going into the restaurant business.

Another undeniable factor in achieving success is luck. There is a lot of truth in the proverbial expression "to be in the right place at the right time." And having bad luck in other aspects of your life—ill health, family problems, and the like—will likely affect your chances of achieving career success. Of course, there are no hard rules about any of this, and we can all point to people who have overcome enormous handicaps and hardships to achieve unparalleled success. Franklin D. Roosevelt was able to become one of our greatest presidents from a wheelchair after all.

Beyond issues of talent and luck, psychological factors affect our ability to achieve success. You may have heard the expression "self-sabotaging," or you may know people who "shoot themselves in the foot." These expressions allude to a person's ability to undermine his or her own success better than anyone else can. Another expression comes to mind— "snatching defeat from the jaws of victory." Why do certain people seem to fear success to the point of putting up their own roadblocks? There can be a range of explanations for such behavior. Sometimes a person may have been raised in a home where the quest for success becomes an enormously pressured, intense, and counterproductive theme. A child growing up in such circumstances may rebel—if only passively—by always holding back from the success that is just within reach. Another reason for fear of success may be that a person comes out of a particular family or even culture where it is regarded as inappropriate for him or her to surpass a parent in terms of tangible success, such as accruing wealth. Or, perhaps most typically, a person might have fears of success because, deep down, he or she feels a certain sense of inadequacy. If that feeling is never dealt with, then the person may shy away from success—or may even indulge in self-sabotage—for fear of being "exposed." It is helpful to have some sense of the ways that we can encourage and discourage success in ourselves. Professional counseling may be warranted in cases where self-knowledge or self-insight may be lacking.

Beyond the factors just mentioned, certain negative behaviors exist that almost all of us engage in at some time or another. It's useful to take a look at these to see to what extent we're vulnerable to them.

Perfectionism

A number of people to whom we spoke cited perfectionism as one of the "success don'ts." Their comments follow:

📞 In my experience working in restaurants, I've found that perfectionism is more of a problem in the back of the house than in the front. I've worked with chefs who have had such ego problems and who've been such control freaks that heaven forbid you should touch their carrot or move their onion. In the front of the house, the feeling that I've encountered has been more about team play. Not that you don't run across perfectionists up front too, but it just hasn't been as much of a problem.

📞 If you ask me, perfectionism goes hand in hand with workaholism. I know what I'm talking about, because at various times in my life, I've been a serious workaholic. When I get infected that way, I step back and tell myself that while I want to do the very best job possible, it's never going to be a "perfect" job. Nobody but nobody does a perfect job. Remember that.

📞 I grew up in a military family. My dad was a lieutenant colonel in the army. Old Spit 'n Polish, my brothers and I used to call him. He's a good guy, but he really made us toe the mark. We had to be able to bounce a dime on our beds—I'm not kidding. So for a long time, I carried around that kind of perfectionism inside of me—the family legacy. Then when I fell in love and married the woman who became my wife, she started to undo a lot of the stuff that my family handed down to me. She taught me that an unmade bed is not necessarily a sign of laziness and moral decay. In fact, an unmade bed could be a sign of great pleasure.

📞 You know, when you think about those Seven Guiding Principles you've set down, the one that immediately jumped out at me was "[Think] Outside [of] the Box." Because of all the boxes in the world, I don't think you'll find one that boxes you in more than perfectionism. It's such a trap. I owe it to my first boss for busting me out of that one. I was a bus boy in a seafood restaurant on the Cape, and I was running around like a chicken without a head, worrying to death that I might do something wrong. One day my boss took me aside and said, "Listen, kid. Relax a little. You'll live longer. You don't have to be perfect. None of us are." It really helped me out.

Procrastination

There is not a lot of room for procrastination in the restaurant field, at least not on a day-to-day basis. There is—or at least there should be—a real "show must go on" mind-set. You've got customers waiting and meals to serve. But procrastination can be a trap in terms of the way you pursue your career over the long run. You may be holding yourself back, and procrastination could very well be your preferred mode of inaction. Let's hear how your fellow restaurant professionals wrestle with this issue:

My mother used to say that procrastination should be my middle name. I have to admit it: she had a point. All through high school, I practiced the fine art of procrastination. I put off assignments whenever and however I could. You should've heard some of the excuses I came up with. During high school, I worked as a waiter at a hotel, and when I graduated—finally—I continued in the job. I procrastinated about moving on with my life, but my boss, who saw something in me that I didn't see in myself, said that I really ought to go back to school because I could make a real career for myself in this field. Finally, I enrolled in community college and went the hospitality route, and now I'm managing a restaurant. It's taken me a while to get where I am because of my procrastinating tendencies, but the good news is that I'm getting better at dealing with it.

I'm the proverbial ostrich that puts its head in the sand. If I don't like something—it could be going to the dentist, it could be asking for a raise—I'll just keep putting it off. I'm just so good at denying. "What cavity? What raise?"

Hey, let's get something straight here. We *all* procrastinate, to some degree or another. It's only human. I mean, maybe there are people who don't, but they're probably the same people who brush after every meal and always hang their clothes up. The important thing is to be able to recognize when you're procrastinating and to take some good, easy, corrective action. For instance, if I'm really dreading a project, like pulling my income taxes together, let's say, I'll find some little bitty part of the job to start with. Maybe it's sharpening pencils. Maybe it's going through one envelope of receipts. I don't know— something! Because whatever it is, I figure it has to be better than just sitting there.

📣 I counter my natural tendency toward procrastination by factoring rewards into every unpleasant job. A few weeks ago, for example, my boss targeted me to write a press release on this upcoming wine tasting we're having at our restaurant. He knows I was an English major in college, so he figures, hey, it's not such a big deal for her. And he's right—it's not such a big deal. But for some reason or other, I've been putting it off. So what I'll do is I'll tell myself that as soon as I finish the article, I can buy myself something that will give me pleasure. A butterscotch sundae . . . a CD . . . a new pair of running shoes. Some little treat that says, "Okay, you did that. You didn't want to do it, but you did it anyway." And it'll feel good.

Game Plans and Mission Statements

If procrastination and perfectionism are two of the "don'ts," then what are some of the "do's"? One "do" that comes to mind is making a game plan and writing a mission statement. These are the sorts of proactive behaviors that can help you accomplish what you've set out to do. Game plans and mission statements have worked well for many in the field:

🕮 I was very resistant to the idea of a game plan and a mission statement. I grew up in a family with parents who were ex-hippies. They owned a natural foods store, and they would have laughed their heads off at something like a game plan or a mission statement. What kind of Establishment thinking is that, they'd want to know. But I took some business courses in college, and I found out just how useful these things can be. You don't have to be General Motors or Kraft to have a mission statement or a game plan. You can just be you and think of your life as a work in progress . . . which is exactly what it is. A game plan can help you find your way, and a mission statement can come in pretty handy if you get lost.

🕮 My parents owned a pancake house in Boise, Idaho, which may not sound like such great shakes, but in fact people in Boise eat a lot of pancakes. Anyway, mom and dad did well enough to give me and my sisters and brothers pretty much everything we ever needed, including good advice, so I tended to listen to what they had to say. One thing they always pushed was a game plan. Dad said it was like a business plan. With a business plan, you've got the mission statement—who are you, and what do you want to achieve?—and the business plan was the map that helps you get from here to there. Dad said everyone should think of himself or herself as a business, with a mission statement, so that you too could get from here to there. Makes sense, no?

✇ A mission statement defines who you are and identifies your goals. It really helps you to see your life in concrete terms. It can be as short as one sentence. In fact, some of the best mission statements are. At the moment, my mission statement says, "I will try to be the most well-organized and ethical restaurant professional that I can be, and I will try to live a healthy and balanced life."

✇ My life has been full of obstacles. That's just the way it is. Some people are really lucky and have a relatively easy ride. Others, like me, have a lot of moguls on our course. My father died when I was six. I broke a hip in a riding accident when I was 14. I got pregnant when I was 17 and had to give the baby up. I've always had to struggle, but that's made me strong. Still, with so many things coming up on me all the time, it sometimes feels easy to lose my way. So while I was still in school, I made up a mission statement, with my teacher's help, and I wrote it down on a 3×5 index card, and I had it laminated—no kidding. I update my statement as time goes on, and every time I do, I get it laminated again, which is a bit of a pain, but the fact is that my mission statement really helps keep me on track. Just knowing I have one makes me feel a lot different than some of my friends who, love them as I do, seem like they couldn't find their way out of a paper bag.

Goal Setting

We said at the top of this chapter that one of the chief factors in determining success is luck. We'll stand by that statement, but we don't want you to get the wrong idea. Success isn't mostly about luck. It's mostly about hard work and dedication and having an eye to the future. Otherwise put, success, to a large degree, is most likely to emerge from the activity of setting goals.

If you've ever been an athlete, you have a clear sense of what a goal is. A goal is putting the football over the line, putting the soccer ball into the net, or sinking the golf ball into the hole. Because these goals are so specific, many athletes find it beneficial to utilize a mode of thinking called "visualization." The act of visualization involves seeing, through mental images, the goal one wishes to attain, thus creating a kind of "rehearsal" of achievement. When visualizing, you "see" yourself kicking the soccer ball into the net, thereby reinforcing your chances of achieving your goal.

Goals that are less tangible than the ones we've just described also can be made easier to attain through visualization. If we have a clear view of what we want to achieve, then we have a better chance of reaching our goals. To get this clearer view, it helps to have an understanding of *motivation*, the force that propels us toward our goals. Motivation essentially comes in two different forms: *extrinsic* and *intrinsic*. Think of extrinsic motivation as doing what you do for the sake of an outside reward. If you give up smoking, your spouse will buy you a new set of golf clubs. If you get all As on your report card, your parents will pay for your car insurance. Get the idea? Intrinsic motivation comes from within. You decide to give up smoking because you know how important it is for you to maintain good health. You do well in school because doing well in school is a value that you have internalized. Intrinsic motivation is usually more long lasting than extrinsic motivation.

Once you have an understanding of motivation, you can begin to focus on the business of setting goals. Let's hear what your fellow professionals have to say on the topic.

📢 If you asked me what my goal was when I first came into this field, I would have said, "To own my own restaurant." Even though that's still my goal, I realize now that it's a long-term goal, and there are a lot of short-term goals that I have to meet before I can realize my long-term goal. Let's say, for instance, that one of my short-term goals is to write a business plan. Let's say that an even shorter short-term goal is to write the mission statement of my business plan. Or I might have a short-term goal of taking a vacation to Cancun. Short-term and long-term goals can stand side by side. There's nothing wrong with that.

📢 When you think of long-term goals, don't just think about tangible things that you can hold in your hand, like the key to a car or the deed to a house.

Long-term goals should also be about the intangible things, like feeling financially independent and secure, if that's what's important to you, or getting into a good long-term relationship, if that's what you value. Some of these goals can take a very long time to achieve, but hey—that's life.

((Q Be realistic when you're setting goals. If you weigh 250 pounds, don't aim to be a jockey. Setting goals for yourself that you're constantly falling short of is a bummer. What do you need that for?

((Q Setting goals is not like building castles in the air. It's not a fantasy game. It should be a very reality-oriented activity. When you identify a goal, you should have some sense of what it will take for you to realize that goal. Will you have to save money? Will you have to develop new skills? Will it require going back to school? Will you need a mentor or some kind of advisor or even a partner? It's up to you to figure it out.

((Q Most people who are super-successful do not stop setting goals for themselves. They keep at it, raising the bar as they go along. So if they become the CEO of a company, they look around to see what other company they can buy, and that way they can become the CEO of a *bigger* company. If they win a tennis tournament, then they set their sights on winning the top four tennis tournaments of the year—the Grand Slam. Really successful people don't rest on their laurels. Then again, you don't want to be the kind of person who's never satisfied with where you've come to. I guess you'd have to call it a delicate balance.

I learned a really good trick in this motivational seminar that I took. I learned that you have a much better chance of meeting your goals if you frame them using positive language. What do I mean by that? Well, think about it. If you've been struggling with losing weight, and you frame your goal negatively— "I'm not going to fail at any more diets"—you may wind up feeling bad about yourself, and you may actually, and ironically, console yourself with food. If, however, you use positive language instead—something like "I'm going to achieve my desired weight by February"— you'll feel motivated and better about yourself and be better equipped to actually do what you set out to do.

One really good piece of advice, folks: let your goals be *your* goals. Seriously. I mean, I know Grandpa Herman always wanted you to be an airline pilot, and Aunt Marie thought you should be a gastroenterologist, and your parents wanted you to be a concert pianist, but this is *your* life, not theirs. *You* need to figure out what your goals are and how to tune out the rest of the flack.

Dealing with Disappointment

Setting goals is a positive and an important activity, but as you know, it is in the nature of setting goals that you will find yourself falling short of them a fair amount of time. You may have a short-term goal of saving $1,000 toward a vacation, and then the alternator on your car goes, and you're in the hole. That's life. Falling short of our long-term goals can be a much more painful process, but that's life too. You may have trained for years to be an Olympic gymnast or a figure skater, and you may have some kind of unfortunate injury that blows that dream out of the water. What then do you do with your goals and your dreams? Can you develop new goals and new dreams, or do you simmer in disappointment that becomes frustration that becomes bitterness? Goals are important, but just as important is the way you cope with not meeting your goals. Your capacity to deal with disappointment will prove key to how successful you are at getting through life. Here are some very valuable thoughts from your colleagues in the field on the subject of disappointment:

❦ Bad things happen. And good things happen. Essentially, even though we set goals and we go about our lives as if we're in control, because that's a good and healthy way to live, we also have to recognize and accept that life is beyond our control. The events of September 11, 2001 reminds us of this, but we can't let uncertainty and anxiety rule us. We have to focus on what's positive in life, and setting goals is one way of doing that.

❦ In Buddhism, there is an orientation toward looking for the gift in any event. Even when the event is bad, the idea is that there is a gift lurking in there somewhere. Let's say, for instance, that you've been fired. We'll raise the ante and say that it happened right before Christmas. You look around, and it seems that everyone in the world is enjoying life but you. At that point, the Buddhists would say to look for the gift.

Maybe if you can achieve some distance from what's happened to you, you can tell yourself that it really was a dead-end job you were in anyway, and it was time to move on. Maybe it's the nudge you need to go back to school. Or maybe the gift is something totally intangible. Maybe if you don't have the money to buy Christmas presents for people because of what's happened, you'll be able to write poems for them instead. It's all about looking for the gift.

✺ Whenever I've been really disappointed about something—losing a job, losing an account, losing money—I try to look at the situation and, very rationally, determine what I did right and what I did wrong. Chances are, I did a little of each. Sometimes when you have a disappointment, you get overwhelmed with all the things you did wrong, and you wind up feeling stupid and guilty. That's rarely the case. That's just skewed vision. Take a few steps back, and tell yourself that it wasn't all bad, and you aren't entirely to blame.

✺ Don't reproach yourself when you've had a disappointment. There are too many people out there who like to gloat over other people's failures—don't do their job. Be kind to yourself. Tell yourself you'll do better next time. Be your own best friend.

A Balanced Life

It's great to set goals, but make sure your goals are balanced. Simply striving for financial independence, for example, at the expense of satisfying personal relationships or healthy living, is probably not going to feel like a good goal in the long run. The idea is to be well rounded in your aspirations. Your fellow professionals speak out on this subject.

◖◗ I confess: I used to be one of the world's worst workaholics. This field tends to breed workaholism. It's the long hours and the pressure—before you know it, you're into this whole macho thing of driving yourself day and night. As a restaurant manager, sure I've got a lot to take care of. You ought to see what's on my plate. But now that I've reached a certain plateau, I like to think that I've developed enough maturity to recognize that it's not only about the work. That's not a way to live your life. Now I make sure that I get to a movie with friends every now and then or go to the beach on a gorgeous day or just lie back some nights and look at the stars. If you can't do that, then what's the point?

◖◗ I grew up in a family where you were expected to achieve. My father was a real taskmaster, and we had to get the grades he wanted and play the sports and do the whole nine yards. I think that's what drove me for a lot of my years, especially in the beginning when I got into the restaurant field, but over time, I began to realize that life wasn't about pleasing my father or living by his standards. It was about finding what works for me. And if I make some mistakes on the way, so be it.

◖◗ All my life I wanted to own my own restaurant and, for the last 10 years, I have. It's a terrific restaurant. It's one of the most popular in DC, and I'm super-proud of what I've accomplished. But there's an old saying: "Watch out what you wish for because it might come true." Now I don't want you to think that I'm not happy with my achievements, because I really am. But the reality is that there's a downside to everything. Now that I've realized my dream, I find myself becoming a kind of money machine. The more hours I put in, the more money I can make. It's gotten so bad that my wife has threatened to leave me if I don't slow down. So I'm trying . . .

📢 I was an assistant manager to this guy who is really some nut. He knows how to manage a restaurant—don't get me wrong—but he's on such a macho, workaholic kick that it'll drive you crazy. And you know what? In my experience, I've found that workaholics really don't get any more done than anybody else. Your basic workaholic is just an obsessive-compulsive personality who takes pleasure in doing things the hard way and who'll make any task look difficult because then they can work harder at it. They're work junkies, and they expect you to be one too.

📢 When I felt like I was getting into a workaholic thing that was interfering with my relationships, I went to see a therapist, and she came up with some behavior modification stuff for me. One of these "new ways of being" that I've learned from her is to take vacations on a regular schedule. For the past two years, I've taken two vacations a year, one in the winter, one in the summer, no matter what's happening. And you know what? I love it! It clears my head, it restores me, it gets me away from the craziness, and it gives me a chance to develop other aspects of myself. Last year, I went snorkeling in Belize. I saw the most amazing fish and marine life. It was like discovering a whole new dimension to this world I live in, and I came away feeling something like joy.

❦ One thing that helps give me balance is that I try to move outside of the world of food as much as I can. I played the clarinet all through high school and college, and now I'm in a wind ensemble. Once a week, we meet, we play, we catch up. There's a history professor on flute, a graphic artist on bassoon, a personal trainer on oboe . . . all these people from different walks of life, and it broadens me so. I love it.

As you can see from this chapter, the business of setting goals can be complicated and has a lot to do with larger feelings about success and motivation and where you stand in the world. Another area of your life as a restaurant professional that is every bit as complicated involves the way you relate to other people, particularly those with whom you work. In the next chapter, we offer insights and advice on how to handle these interpersonal issues.

Chapter 4

Go, Team!

Industrial psychologists use a word to describe the dynamic of workers in any given situation. They call it a "system." Every work situation has its own system. A lighthouse presents a very uncomplicated system: there's the lighthouse itself, and then there's the lighthouse keeper. A mom-and-pop candy store has a somewhat more complicated system . . . particularly if mom and pop are not getting along so well. A firehouse is an even more complicated system, but the fact that it is made up mostly of men in a very structured hierarchy means that it is not as complicated as many other systems can be. A real estate office is an example of a system that can be extremely complicated, with men and women competing for properties that translate into commissions. There is so much opportunity for rivalries and backstabbing in that kind of system that people sometimes think of it as a shark tank. And then there are restaurants. Which kind of system do you think your average restaurant represents? Rather complicated? We agree.

Although everyone in the restaurant is more or less working toward a common purpose—to prepare and serve food for customers that will induce them to return to the restaurant—all kinds of complications can arise. Chief among these is the traditional rivalry between the front of the house and the back of the house. Other complications involve issues of gender, age, culture, and economics. The restaurant also becomes a complicated system by the stress and pressure factored into the environment. Compare a restaurant to a dress shop, for instance. Although there are pressures in a dress shop too— merchandise has to move, after all—there is not the ongoing, day-to-day, night-to-night issue of performing at your peak. Falling down on the job in a restaurant can very well translate into a lost customer. Too many lost customers will mean no more restaurant. You do the math.

So when you take into account the issues just mentioned, you will no doubt agree that the restaurant arena is full of potential land mines. Like most systems, there is a hierarchy, and the effectiveness of this hierarchy will determine to a large degree the success of the entire system. Most people would agree that in a restaurant, as in any system, there are real top-down issues in place, and that strength at the top—or weakness—will be felt all the way through the system.

The system that many businesses try to use as a model for success is the team. If you've never been an athlete, don't panic. You can do just fine. But if you have been an athlete, then you know why the team is looked to as a shining example of how people can work together. A good team has a strong leader at the helm—call him or her "the coach." A good coach is fair and does not play favorites. A good coach knows the game. He or she can help each player realize his or her personal best. A good coach also helps players deal with inevitable disappointments. Each player on the team works at honing individual skills, but each player also is part of something bigger. This means that a player who has mastered a particular skill often will help another player who is not quite there. It also means that players realize that when they have disputes they cannot act out on them without inhibition for that will threaten the team as a whole. And, each player understands that he or she will do his or her best when the team works *as a whole*.

A team can be a beautiful thing, or it can be a chronically losing proposition. Later in this book, we focus on specific ways that managers, owners, and supervisors can function as great coaches for their players, and how waitstaff, bartenders, cashiers, maître d's, and all of the other individual players can help make the team a winner. In this chapter, however, we look at some of the universal behaviors that can help each and every one of us do our best in a team situation. We offer useful tips and strategies from fellow restaurant professionals on everything from conflict resolution to anger management to the giving and receiving of criticism to issues of diversity and gender and more. Let's dig in, shall we?

Learning to Communicate

We're going to start with the biggest issue first: communication. Without good communication, you're not going to have a working team—*period*. We're hard pressed to think of any system where communication is more vital than in the restaurant setting. The front of the house has to communicate with each other, with the customers, and with the back of the house. If that communication doesn't happen, there is little chance for success. The woman who ordered the Arctic char will be given the filet mignon, while the man who ordered filet mignon will get the vegetarian lasagna. Is that going to make your customers happy? We don't think so. We begin by looking at some of the really fundamental issues around communication. Let's hear from your fellow restaurant professionals.

⦿ I manage a large restaurant in Shaker Heights, Ohio, and if you ask me what I think is the most important point to make about communication, I'd have to say that the number 1 thing to remember is that everybody is entitled to a voice. There needs to be total equality when it comes to communication. That doesn't mean that there's going to be equality about the decision making—I'm the manager and the buck stops with me—but my waitstaff and my bartender and my cashier and everybody else on my staff [need] to feel that when they speak, they're going to be heard. And they are.

🕮 I'm a waiter in a restaurant in Dallas. I've been there for four years, and for the most part, I'm okay with it. But our maître d' drives me a little crazy, because he's one of those people who never lets you finish a sentence. As soon as you start to talk, he finishes for you. He really doesn't hear.

🕮 Whenever we get a new kid in to wait tables, I try to teach them that there's a lot of communication that goes on without anything spoken at all. I tell them that you need to be sensitive to the facial expressions and body language of your fellow workers and especially those of your customers. If a customer makes a face, what does that mean? Can you interpret that expression? Is something too hot? Too cold? Is there a lot of shifting and fidgeting, suggesting some kind of discomfort? These kids need to know that unspoken communication can telegraph even more quickly than spoken communication.

🕮 When you think about communication, what immediately comes to mind are the words that people say to one another. Then you start getting into things like gestures and body language and all that. But there are other factors that influence the quality of your communication with another person. For instance, there's your tone of voice. Are you a mumbler? Do you speak in a monotone? Do you go over to a table, and do you make incredible dishes sound like corned beef hash? Are you loud, grating, strident? Ask yourself these questions, or better yet, ask them of someone you really trust. Then *do* something about it.

◖◗ Listening is so important. Sometimes I'll have someone on my staff that's just not a good listener at all. Now it's a very human response, when someone's not listening to you, for you to feel insulted and angry. What is this person saying? That I'm boring? Not worth listening to? But you should always step back from that gut response and instead first find out if there's some physiological reason why this person can't seem to hear you. Maybe she just doesn't hear very well. I had a cashier working for me who, it turned out, had a serious hearing deficit that she had been in the act of denying for a long time. Once she got a hearing aid, our relationship improved enormously.

◖◗ Communication is a two-way street. One person talks, the other listens, and then usually you switch roles. In other words, listening should not be a totally passive behavior. If I'm working with someone who never asks questions and has very little to say, it's not easy for me to become interested in that person.

◖◗ Some of my staff act like children—they really do. We have staff meetings where we talk about the importance of good communication, and then they come running over to me when I'm up to my elbows in problems and they start asking about a raise or a day off so they can go to their high school reunion. People really need to use their heads and pick a decent time to communicate.

As a manager, I've been to many different seminars that present many different managerial tools, and one particularly valuable thing that I came away with from one of these seminars was an understanding of what's called "reflective listening." This is when somebody tells you something and you basically tell it back to them, so that everyone's on the same page, and you know the thing's been said. For instance, let's imagine that my owner says to me, "We need new table linens." I will reply, "Yes. I agree. We need new table linens. What did you have in mind?" This is my way of nailing down what he's said to me, so that there is no confusion. It's a very useful kind of strategy, but of course you don't want to do it all the time. I mean, you don't want to sound like a parrot, after all. Just save it for the important stuff.

Popeye, Anyone?

In certain restaurant situations, such as busy diners and lunch counters, the pace gets so intense at times that every second counts, and communication is key. That's how "diner talk" came about. Just for fun, have a look at some of the following coded communications from the glory days of the diner:

Diner Talk	Plain English
Adam and Eve on a raft	Two poached eggs on toast
Baled hay	Shredded wheat
B and B	Bread and butter

C. J. White	Cream cheese and jelly on white bread
Cowboy with spurs	Western omelet with French fries
Cremate it	Toast the bread
Flop two	Two fried eggs, over easy
Hold the grass	Sandwich without lettuce
Joe/Java	Coffee
Lighthouse	Bottle of ketchup
Nervous pudding	Jello
Popeye	Spinach
Put a hat on it	Add ice cream
Sneeze	Pepper
Vermont	Maple syrup
Wimpy	Hamburger

Personality and Attitude

Along with good communication skills, another issue that impacts on your ability to function as part of a team is your very personality and attitude. You're not really going to be able to change your personality, but there's no reason you can't make some necessary attitude adjustments. Let's listen to what your fellow restaurant professionals have to say about this.

✆ Growing up as the only girl in a family with four brothers, I learned how to take care of myself. That's come in handy in the restaurant world where people don't always say "Please?," "May I?," and "Thank-you." I work with a girl who's really shy and introverted, and a lot of times she gets lost in the shuffle. It's a grabby world, and she doesn't grab.

✆ No matter how much of a shrinking violet you may be, we can all become better at putting ourselves forward. It's called "assertiveness training", and it's something you need to learn how to do. Just remember that being assertive and aggressive are two different things. You don't ever have to be aggressive or pretend that you're Vin Diesel or whatever. You can still be the same nice, gentle, kind person you've always been. But you do have to be assertive, meaning that you can't let people walk over you. When they do, you have to be able to tell them to stop, and you have to be able to ask for what you want. And remember—being assertive makes life easier for the people you work with. Being passive and withdrawn and keeping your feelings to yourself makes life harder for everyone, particularly you.

✆ I grew up in a family where the only colors in the crayon box were black and shades of gray. Birthdays and Christmas were "so much work." You could get killed riding a bike and drown from swimming. You know what I mean? (Hopefully you don't.) Growing up this way made me very susceptible to depression and anxiety and very prone to

Assertiveness: The Short Version

Entire books have been written about assertiveness, and some of them can be very useful, but we'd like to leave you with a quick, three-step strategy with which to approach the issue. It's a very simple idea, but it works.

1. Begin with *I feel*. "I *feel* like you're using me as a punching bag." "I *feel* passed over for other people."

2. Move on to *I want*. "I *want* to be treated with respect and consideration." "I *want* to be noticed and acknowledged just like the others are."

3. End with *I will*. "I *will* let you know when I think I'm being treated disrespectfully, and I *will* expect you to own up to it." "I *will* be asking you for regular reviews so that I can get an ongoing assessment of my performance."

This simple, three-step process can go a long way toward getting you out of a pattern that doesn't feel right.

taking things much harder than I needed to and overreacting all over the place. I went into therapy, and one of the things I took away from that experience was a coping strategy called "reframing." With reframing, you learn how to look at an event from another vantage point. For instance, if my boss tells me that "business is bad," instead of going to the place of gloom and doom that I learned to live in from my childhood—"We're going to have to close down; We're going to lose our jobs"—I try to look at it from another perspective. I'll tell myself, "Okay, this is a problem, and I'll try to come up with a solution. Maybe we need to come up with some new marketing plans. Maybe we have to cut corners." Reframing just gives you a different orientation.

📢 I have a very friendly, open, outgoing personality. My mom calls me "Little Mary Sunshine" (I know—gag me). But I've had to learn to check some of my impulses. A restaurant is a very closed world. You're with the same group of people day and night; you're often eating together. You can't be so naïve as to think that you can be friends with everyone, so you have to watch what you say. Very important: loose lips sink ships. Don't go around blabbing personal information or information about anyone else. That's called "gossip," and [it comes] back to haunt you. Gossiping is a sure way to get cut from the team.

📢 Being on a team means helping the people you work with. If you know something that somebody else doesn't know—how to fold a napkin right; how to describe the difference between a chardonnay and a sauvignon blanc—don't keep it to yourself. This isn't a contest, with everyone out to cover his or her own behinds. This is a team, or at least it should be, where everyone pulls together.

Conflict Resolution

As you can tell from the aforementioned, even Little Mary Sunshine has her moments when she feels betrayed, angry, confused, and ill treated. No matter how well you get along with other people, there will still come a time when you've angered someone or someone has angered you. That's life. You can't be a hothouse flower who never feels the cold winds and blazing heats that criss-cross the real world. The question is: What do you do about it when you get into a conflict? Is it suddenly World War III? Do you aim your cannon at the enemy and blow off both barrels? Do you threaten to jump off a parapet? Do you engage in guerilla warfare and sabotage?

If your answer to any of these questions is affirmative, then you're doing something wrong. Anger should not incite lunacy. Anger should be recognized as a reality in your life—indeed, in the lives of us all—and one that can, if handled correctly, even lead to improved communication. The way to manage conflict, both on the job and off, is through *conflict resolution*. Without it—which we can define as "the means by which to negotiate differences and come to some form of mutual agreement"— the tensions and bad feelings that can develop may linger to produce even deeper rifts. Let's hear how your fellow restaurant professionals approach conflict resolution:

As a manager, I push conflict resolution all the time. We talk about it regularly in our restaurant, because it's amazing how quickly some of these conflicts can totally spiral out of control. We've got a few particularly volatile personalities working for us who, to borrow a kitchen phrase, are masters at throwing fat on the fire. The thing that I always stress about conflict is that it's a two-way street, and you have to figure out what your part is in it. Passive people contribute to conflicts just as aggressive people do. So start by asking yourself what you bring to the table. Are you terribly sensitive? The sort of person that if somebody looks at you the wrong way you burst into tears? Do you like to play one person against another? Or are you rigid and inflexible and always insistent on being right? Ask yourself these questions, and then ask other people to give you their input, and when you've collected the data, see what kind of personal changes you're ready to make.

🔊 The most important factor in conflict resolution is commitment. Everybody involved has to be committed to getting beyond the problem. If you're all equally committed to getting beyond it, it will happen.

🔊 Listening is key to conflict resolution. Some people are just yellers and screamers, and they never listen. Those people have to be held accountable for their behavior. You may have to take them aside—even a group of you—and let them know that they have to find other ways to express themselves.

🔊 Very important: treat each conflict as a solitary event. Don't let yourself get into this thing where you're always looking for patterns and reconstructing your history. As soon as you go back to conflicts in the past, you're sunk. If I'm having an issue with a coworker and I start saying things like "What about that time I asked you to fill in for me when I was going to my sister's wedding, and you said you would and then you left me in the lurch?" Well, guess what? We're going to be right back in that old fight within two minutes flat. Don't go there!

 Don't worry about "winning" a fight. There should be no "winners" and "losers" when it comes to conflicts. Instead, think of a conflict as a problem that two people share. Turn to the person you're having the conflict with and say, "Jean, let's you and I figure a way out of this mess, okay?" Enlist the other person. Make it collaborative. It's a powerful message.

 Here's a neat trick that somebody taught me: when you're trying to resolve a conflict, always use the name of the person you're having the conflict with. "Jenny, you seem upset." "Marc, why don't we talk about this?" "Fritz, we seem to be having a lot of problems with each other lately." The use of the name signifies that you see the other person as a person, not as an enemy, and that goes a long way toward patching things up.

Anger Management

It's great to have conflict resolution in your tool chest, but a lot of conflicts can be avoided if you, as an individual, develop the ability to manage your anger. Keep in mind that there are different kinds of anger styles, and that they can all be destructive. The most visible and scary is the road rage variety, where the person just explodes, and the outcome can actually be violent. Such people often are deeply disturbed, and their need for anger management is just part of a broader need to adjust their entire personality. Other people have passive or passive-aggressive styles of anger. They don't seem to "do" anything, but they can inspire huge amounts of anger by "acting out" in ways such as being late, forgetting responsibilities, breaking important equipment, and so on. People with these anger styles are tough to deal with, because they're usually masters of denial. What is your anger style, and how well do you manage your anger? Consider these tips from your fellow restaurant professionals:

❧ I grew up terrified by anger. My father was an alcoholic, and he would go into terrible rages. My sister and my mother and I tiptoed through life like three little mice. It wasn't until I was fully an adult that I could even begin to allow myself to feel anger. After a lot of work, I now recognize that anger is a totally normal part of life. I can now "take my temperature" in a charged situation and ask myself, "Am I annoyed? Irritated? Really upset? In a rage?" (To tell you the truth, I've never been in a rage. I guess you could say I'm working toward it.)

❧ Anger and fights are painful, so I try my best to avoid them. For instance, I used to get into arguments with my teenage daughter about the way she kept her room. Then I came to the realization that these fights were taking a lot out of our relationship, so I just told her to keep her door closed. The less I see, the better I am at keeping the peace.

📞 Do you know the old bit about counting to 10 when you're angry? Guess what? It helps. So does deep breathing. So does walking away. Anything to break the pattern.

📞 Do everybody a favor and steer clear of words like "never" or "always." As in, "You *never* do anything right," or "I'm *always* waiting for you." Those words are like little daggers; they cause wounds, and wounds take a long time to heal.

📞 An important thing to remember with regard to anger is whatever is said cannot be unsaid. If you turn to someone and say, "I hate you, I've always hated you, and I always *will* hate you," it's hard to get beyond that when things calm down a little. Even worse is putting it in writing. Now don't get me wrong—I couldn't live without e-mail—but I've noticed in a number of situations where people write these terrible e-mails to each other, and then they're there, as a historical record, never to be forgotten.

📞 Look, just because somebody gets angry with you and acts out, that doesn't mean you have to meet that person in that place. *Not* rising to the occasion and locking horns really isn't at all wimpy. You can turn the other cheek. You can walk away from somebody who's screaming and ranting and say, "That person is out of control," or "That person seems to be having a very bad day." Try it some time. You'll see how right it feels.

Feedback and Criticism

An important aspect of functioning on a team is being able to give and receive criticism and feedback. Even when feedback is couched in supportive terms, it is still difficult for most of us to accept criticism without characterizing it as negative. It is crucial to get beyond this attitude, however, for if you are unable to receive constructive criticism, you may find it difficult to grow. Let's hear what some of your fellow restaurant professionals have to say on the subject.

🌊 Part of having a positive attitude is being able to handle criticism. My father was always very critical of me, so criticism was something I saw as a very negative thing, and I've had to work really hard to become better at accepting it. I used to withdraw or rationalize or try to blame other people whenever I was criticized, but now I've come to learn that the best way to handle criticism is to see it as a positive thing. It's feedback that can teach you how to become better at what you're trying to do.

🌊 Sometimes I just want to sit my staff down and explain how it works. "Look, folks, I'm the manager. It's my *job* to tell you when something you're doing could be improved upon." Let me give you an example. I have a lovely young woman on staff. She just graduated from college and she's waiting tables till she figures out what she wants to do with her life. Not a problem. I'm not expecting every member of my wait-staff to turn his or her lives over to me. I understand that waiting tables is a transitional position for some people. But she'll tell this to everybody she waits on. It's like, "Hello, my name is Marcie and I'm your wait-ress tonight and I'm just doing this till I decide if I want to become a social worker or a physician's assistant." So I call her over one night and say, "Marcie, you don't have to get so personal with everyone." And before I know it, she's crying. I mean, come *on*.

📖 Being part of a team means that when you're letting the team down in some way, you're told as much. I had a bartender who was always showing up late. Other people had to cover for him. I told him he either had to clean up his act or find another job. That's called "feed-back." It's not wrapped all pretty with a bow, but I told him the truth and nothing but. To his credit, he did clean up his act, and he's still with us. He knew how to take criticism without becoming all defensive and resentful.

📖 I was an assistant manager to a man who's very well known and much beloved in the field. He's a real-ly kind person, but also really strong. One of the things he taught me was that you don't criticize people for things they can't change. If someone is high-strung, don't get on his case because he isn't mellow. If some-one is a slow and deliberate learner, don't criticize him for not being a quick study. In other words, work with what you've got, reinforce the merits and accom-plishments of that person, and tactfully, gently, and sensitively introduce ideas for how that person can improve performance.

🔊 I'm the hostess in a very upscale, cantina-style Mexican restaurant in Scottsdale, Arizona. I like my job because I like people. I get to greet them, and for me it's a pleasure to see people out enjoying themselves. Before I did this, I worked in child care, which I also loved, but the money just wasn't there. Still, while I was in that world, I learned something that I think is useful to remember when you're involved in what you're calling "team play." Working with children, I learned to always use "I" instead of "you," as in "I feel sad when you break a toy" instead of "Look how you broke that!" When you talk about your own feelings and responses, it's a lot better than attributing things to the other person.

🔊 People don't really believe this, but as a manager I find it almost as hard to give negative feedback as the other person has receiving it. As an assistant manager, I had to learn the skill of giving negative feedback and not feeling like I was betraying someone or damaging someone's reputation. I was just very invested in being a real Mr. Nice Guy. Then one of my staff—an older woman—came to me and said, "Aren't you ever going to tell me how I'm *really* doing?" That made me realize that I wasn't doing anyone a favor by being so nice. My staff didn't need smiles and hugs, although there's nothing wrong with those. But what they really needed was the truth, even if the truth is sometimes hard to hear.

The Front of the House Versus the Back of the House

In a restaurant, the kitchen staff, as you know, is often referred to as "the back of the house," while the service staff is called "the front of the house." It is not uncommon for these two groups to think of themselves as two distinct teams engaged in intramurals with each other. In the most successful and smoothly operating establishments, however, there is a healthy integration and interface between the two groups. Our restaurant professionals had some interesting things to say about this topic:

The waitstaff in our restaurant turns over a portion of their gratuities for the kitchen staff once a week. It doesn't amount to all that much, but this is really a case of where the gesture goes a very long way. I've worked in many restaurants where a real animosity built up between the two camps over the issue of gratuities, and here my kitchen staff really feels good about this gesture. They respond by often sharing with the waitstaff the special foods, wines, and other promotional items that come through the kitchen. It's a "you scratch my back, I'll scratch yours" kind of mentality.

I manage a restaurant in downtown Minneapolis. It's a very sleek, beautiful new restaurant in one of the most exciting office complexes in the city, and one of the things I particularly love about the design is that we've got an open kitchen. Not only does that break down the "them against us" feeling you sometimes get between the front and the back of the house, but it really cuts down on slammed doors.

 One of the best ways to foster a healthy relationship between the front and the back is by instituting cross-training in your restaurant. We've done it in ours. Our servers learn basic procedures and timing in the kitchen by doing a stint on line or at the cold station, while we put the line cooks out in front to run food or greet guests in the dining room. That way, everybody's up on what everyone else does. There's no mystery and no special sense of entitlement anywhere.

 You can do the same kinds of things that people do in offices and corporations all over the world in your restaurant. On days off, we schedule special outings. We might go to a vineyard or have a picnic at the beach. A few weeks ago, we all went to see this new goat cheese operation that opened up in the countryside. That kind of activity can go a long way toward team building, and team building goes a long way toward achieving success.

Gender Issues

Gender has always been an issue in the restaurant world. Once upon a time, there were no waitresses to be found in fine restaurants. It was considered a man's job. Obviously if there were no waitresses, then there would be no women restaurant managers. There were always women who owned restaurants, and some were great entrepreneurial figures, such as Sylvia, of the legendary restaurant Sylvia's in Harlem, who spun off a line of supermarket products that has proven to be highly successful, or Elaine Kaufman, whose restaurant/bar, Elaine's, in New York City became the famous watering hole for people such as Woody Allen and Alec Baldwin. Over the last decade or so, the situation for women has changed dramatically in the restaurant field. In a 1992 poll, 60 percent of employees in the restaurant industry were women, and almost 30 percent of all cooking school students were women. But gender issues are still at play in the restaurant field, as they are in every field. They will never go away, but our awareness of how to handle them will hopefully become ever more sophisticated.

Women in Power

Many cultural myths and unwritten rules affect the way women—and men—feel about women in power. Powerful women often are seen as being overly ambitious, manipulative, and power hungry, whereas men in power are seen in much more positive terms, as strong and decisive and highly attractive. Our restaurant professionals deal with this issue in the following ways:

❦ I work as a maître d' in a restaurant in Chicago. I've had managers who are men, and now I have a manager who's a woman, and I have to say I prefer working for a woman at this point. This surprised me, because at first I had a lot of preconceptions about what it would be like. I thought a woman would be weaker, less likely to call the shots, and we'd be twisting in the wind. But then I said to myself, "Wait a minute. Golda Meir was a woman. Indira Gandhi was a woman. Margaret Thatcher was a woman. They ran *countries*. Surely this woman can run a restaurant." And the fact is, she can. I don't want to generalize to all women on the basis of this one experience, but so far I've found that Linda is more compassionate and more concerned with how people are feeling than the men I've worked for have been. And she's just as efficient. In short, I think she's terrific.

◖ I'm a banquet manager for a hotel in San Francisco. It's a big job with a lot of pressure. I can handle it. But I have to say that I've known very few women, myself included, who feel totally natural and comfortable in a position of power. Not that we can't hold positions of power and hold them every bit as well as men do, but you have to recognize that it's a stretch for most of us. Giving orders and running the show doesn't come naturally to most women, Judge Judy aside. Still, it feels good to stretch.

◖ I'm a woman who works for a woman—she's the manager, and I'm the assistant manager for a restaurant in Miami—and I've got to say that she's really a little too soft. She likes to be liked. I think a lot of women are like that. I'm not so much. I grew up the only girl in a family of five boys, and I guess I think more like a man. In other words, I don't care that much about being liked.

🔊 I was an athlete in college—I did crew, all four years—and I think that experience, which so many men take for granted, is great for a woman to have. Being on a sports team allows you to learn how to interact easily with other people. It's that locker room thing. You learn how to crack jokes and snap towels. So many women in power tend to get very serious and lose the fun part of it. When you're at the top, you've got to remember how to laugh and not be so defensive.

Sexual Harassment

Sometimes things come along that drastically disrupt any sense of team building. One such "thing" is sexual harassment. What is it exactly, and what can you do about it?

🔊 Sexual harassment comes in a lot of different forms. It can be a remark or a pattern of making remarks that makes you feel uncomfortable. If your boss says to you, "Oh, you look amazing today. You really know how to work it," that's not a compliment if it doesn't feel to you like a compliment (and don't let anybody convince you that it *should* feel like a compliment). Comments about your hair, your clothes, your shoes, your fingernails— that's nobody's business but your own.

🔊 Lots of people who indulge in sexual harassment do so very knowingly and with great calculation. They see it as a kind of seduction, a cat-and-mouse game. One day it's "Oh, don't you look nice." The next day it's "You really know how to wear red." A week later it's "Here comes the lady in red." It's something that you've really got to nip in the bud early on.

✆ Don't expect your harasser to stop on his own. You know when he'll stop? When you let him know that you have zero tolerance for what he's doing.

✆ What I'm about to say goes for everyone. Don't put yourself in a vulnerable position. If someone puts out something that causes your antennae to go up, don't go out to lunch, just the two of you. Don't come in early or stay late if that means you're going to be alone with that person. This goes for whether you're the person who may be harassed or whether you're the person who might be unfairly accused of harassing.

✆ If you've been harassed, chances are other people in your place of work have been harassed as well. Sexual harassers are usually serial offenders. Ask around very carefully—you don't want to slander someone—to see if you pick up any vibes from anyone else that may have been victimized.

✆ Report harassment *immediately* to your supervisor. If your supervisor *is* the harasser, and there's nowhere higher to go, talk to an attorney.

✆ Look, let's get real here. If you're being harassed, you may have to quit your job. Whether you will wind up getting any legal satisfaction or not ultimately is a whole other story. The important thing to keep in mind is that you mustn't let yourself remain in a position in which you are being victimized. There are other jobs out there. Nothing is worth that.

The Diverse Workplace

You'll rarely find work worlds that are as culturally diverse as the restaurant field. A lot of entry-level positions in the field, such as dishwashers, for instance, attract recent immigrants. The high end—that is, super chefs—also attracts an international contingent. If you're working in a big city, expect to be working alongside men and women from the European Union, from Asia, from South and Central America, and from Africa. This diversity can be tremendously interesting, but it also may be something of a challenge to navigate. Some thoughts from restaurant professionals follow:

I came to America from Brazil eight years ago, and it's a fabulous country! The only trouble is that a lot of Americans act like it's the *only* country in the world, and it's not.

As an American who has traveled all over the world, I see how guilty we are of ethnocentricity. That means thinking that your culture is the only culture in the world. We have to remember that the things we value so much in our culture, like speed and punctuality and everything fast, fast, fast, may not be such a big deal in other parts of the world.

Part of what we do to build a team around here is that we don't make jokes about anybody from any ethnic group. It's not allowed. Simple as that. Those jokes reinforce mindless stereotype.

📞 Here's a pointer: people who are not native English speakers are not deaf. You do not have to speak to them *in a very loud voice*. Okay?

We've covered quite a lot about team building here. In our next chapter, we focus on ways to take care of yourself and how to stay healthy and sane.

Chapter Reference

Dornenburg, Andrew and Page, Karen. (2003). *Becoming a chef*. Hoboken, NJ: John Wiley & Sons.

Chapter 5

The Whole You

Working in a restaurant, you probably already have a sense of how poorly some people treat their bodies. How many of your customers overeat and drink too much? Maybe these customers are a restaurant owner's dream, but let's face it, it's disturbing to see people abuse their bodies, isn't it?

How about you? How well are you taking care of yourself? This chapter is all about *wellness*, which is so important if you are going to be able to achieve your potential and realize success. Wellness is connected to *wholeness*, by which we mean seeing yourself as a being whose parts are closely interconnected. The word "holistic" derives from the idea of wholeness, and a holistic sensibility underlies this chapter. We believe that the mind influences the workings of the body, and the body influences the workings of the mind. Pacing yourself, learning how to deal with disappointment and stress, adopting behaviors that make the most of your energy and that protect you against exhaustion, and more will be covered in this important chapter.

As a restaurant professional, you have found yourself in a work situation that can present multiple challenges to wellness. Restaurants can be dangerous places, ripe for unfortunate encounters with heavy pots, hot stoves, sharp equipment, and bad microbes if not carefully monitored. Your work also may make arduous physical demands on you, such as lifting, bending down, and reaching, and, at the very least, you're almost sure to be on your feet for the better part of the day. What's more, you are working under the stress of performance pressure. That means long hours, and long hours can lead to sleep deprivation. The fact that you're surrounded by food and drink also can tempt you to overindulge. Yipes—you're working in a minefield!

Seriously though, restaurants, like all work situations, offer their share of pitfalls. To ensure your health and well-being, it is best to act preventively rather than reactively. In other words, dealing with a problem *after* the fact is far more complicated and difficult than dealing with it *before* the fact. In this chapter, we identify areas of risk and offer strategies to help you avoid those risks. And what better place to begin than with food?

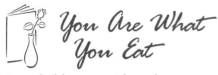

You Are What You Eat

It's probably no accident that you wound up in the restaurant business. A lot of what attracted you might very well have been the food. And why not? Food is one of life's greatest pleasures, after all. Purple plums, red tomatoes, napoleons, fresh-baked loaves of bread . . . food is a feast for the senses, beautiful to look at, wonderful to smell, and delicious. It's also one of life's absolute necessities, for food is the fuel that keeps us going. So with all of the positive vibes around food, how do so many strange and negative messages get thrown into the mix?

Food, in fact, often becomes the bane of people's existence. Obesity has become epidemic in our nation, and eating disorders such as anorexia and bulimia also are rampant. We live in the richest society in history, but we have affluent youngsters who are literally starving themselves to death. Let's listen to what fellow restaurant professionals have to say on the subject of food in general.

My work as a restaurant consultant has taken me to a great many foreign nations, principally in Europe. I've spent months at a time in France and Italy and Spain, and one thing that always strikes me when I'm over there is that people rarely eat to excess. They adore food, and you want to die for their cheeses and breads and wines, but they don't abuse any of it. They seem to naturally eat well-balanced, well-proportioned meals of healthy food. Here at home, on the other hand, so many people are trapped in a sick relationship with food. We have people who come to our restaurant, literally gorging themselves on our food, and then ask for doggie bags to bring home whatever their friends haven't finished. And what about the people who come in and ask for a lettuce leaf only or a few sprouts because heaven forbid they should ingest more than 12 calories? There's so much craziness out there about food.

✊ One of the scariest words in the English language is "supersize." When I see kids walking around with 64-ounce plastic containers of soda, I have to stop and wonder which planet I'm visiting.

✊ My ex-wife used to drive me crazy when it came to food. She was like this coy little girl, turning all these foods into forbidden fruit. She'd always have just a "teensy-tiny" piece of chocolate, please, or an "itty-bitty" slice of cake. I'd tell her that it wasn't going to bite her. The idea was for *her* to bite *it*.

✊ The biggest scam going is the whole low-fat/no-fat thing. Suddenly people are absolutely phobic about fat. It's like, don't come near me with that butter! Since when did fat become a four-letter word? Fat is actually good for you in certain amounts, and certain kinds of fat, like those you get from nuts and olive oil and avocados, are *very* good for you. Fat also makes food taste wonderful. When I see things like no-fat pasta dishes, I want to cry. How can you eat pasta without some oil on it? Okay—maybe if you have a serious medical condition and you're absolutely forbidden to eat fat for some reason, that's one thing. But as a lifestyle choice? It's nuts . . . you should pardon the expression.

Watching Your Weight

"I was working in this amazing German restaurant in Milwaukee," recalls Fred, now a banquet manager in Richmond, Virginia. "There were foods I never ate before. Sauerbraten, wiener schnitzel, weisswurst, apfelkuchen—and I fell in love with it all. It was so heavy and rich and incredibly satisfying. But I put on pounds like you wouldn't believe. And I was barely paying attention. Before I knew it, I couldn't close my pants. Being around food like that is definitely a real occupational hazard."

How can you find your way past the pitfalls of an irresistible kitchen? Some strategies follow from fellow culinary professionals:

One way to start navigating the whole weight issue is to understand something about the physiology and the psychology of hunger. There's more than one kind of hunger. There's stomach hunger, when you haven't eaten for seven or eight hours, and your belly starts bellyaching. Then there's mouth hunger, like when you smell fresh bread or Chinese food and your mouth screams, "I want that! I want that!" Then there's the hunger that's inspired by emotional needs, when you feel anxious or depressed or empty and you want to "fill yourself up." Sorting out these various kinds of hunger and getting yourself to eat only when you feel stomach hunger is a big step in your campaign to get your weight issue under control.

✺ I waitress in this sort of trendy little diner in Brooklyn called "Mom's." We serve all the retro foods like meat loaf and macaroni and cheese and rice pudding and all the things that mother used to make if mother didn't just pop a TV dinner in the oven like my mother did. Anyway, right after September 11, when a lot of restaurants in New York City were losing their shirts, we were packed. We had customers lining up to get in, and over the next few months, I watched our regulars start to pack on the pounds. All that comfort food was taking its toll on them. Eating for emotional needs can be pretty dangerous.

✺ Sometimes I'll watch our customers eating, and they're forking the food down so fast that they're not even tasting it. They don't give their brains a chance to catch up with their mouths, so they don't feel satisfied after they eat. Eating slowly is a great way to get your appetite under control. Remember what your mother said about chewing each bite 50 times (or was it 25¢)? She was right. It's good for the digestion (you'll have a lot less gas), and it gives you a chance to satisfy yourself.

✺ You can help curb your appetite just by drinking a lot of water. Drink a few glasses before a meal. It fills you up, so you won't have to take in as many solids.

Don't Forget to Hydrate

We don't want to shock you, but your body is made up of 60 to 70 percent water. When you lose some of that water—through sweating, through excreting, and so on—you have to replenish it. If you don't, you'll be opening yourself up to fatigue and much worse symptoms, especially dehydration. Your colleagues in the field understand just how important water really is:

🌀 You know the expression, "If you can't stand the heat, get out of the kitchen"? Well, it gets pretty darned hot in the front of the house too. Why? Because you're dealing with the customers! You think that's easy? I can work up a sweat just *thinking* about customers. So when I sweat, I drink.

🌀 Do yourself a favor: drink *before* you get thirsty. You'll have to drink twice as much to catch up if you allow dehydration to set in.

🌀 I don't go anywhere without my water. It's second nature with me.

🌀 Okay, so maybe you're thinking it's not the *water* that's important, it's the *liquid*. And if that's the case, then you might just as well enjoy your double mochaccino lattés or whatever, right? Wrong. Some liquids, like coffee and tea, can act as diuretics, actually causing water to *leave* your body. Other liquids, like soda pop and bottled shakes and juices, are often filled with unnecessary calories or, as in the case of power drinks, unnecessary chemicals. What's as cheap, healthy, non-fattening, and refreshing as water? Not a thing, so drink up.

🕭 Water's great, but like almost anything else in the world, you can overdo it too. I've heard of people who were drinking, like, gallons of water a day, and that can flush minerals and vitamins out of your system and can actually send you into shock.

Dieting

What's a multibillion dollar industry that essentially provides the consumer with very few results? You've got it—the diet industry. The subject certainly fired up our restaurant professionals:

🕭 If there's one word I hate, it's "diet." There isn't a night that I'm waiting on people when I'm not told that so and so and such and such are on a diet. Like I care? Okay, it's one thing if somebody has to be on a *special* diet. If you're a diabetic or have high blood pressure or whatever. But when some woman who's a size two is telling me she's watching her weight, it's like, *give me a break, lady.*

🌀 I just found out about the best diet in the world. It's better than the grapefruit diet, the cabbage soup diet, the Scarsdale diet, or the Atkins diet. It's the "eat less" diet. Seriously. Cut your portions in half, and watch the pounds melt away. And when you add regular exercise, the results are amazing.

🌀 You want to know the engine that drives the diet industry? It's the advertising industry. Those guys are out to make us all totally crazy about the way our bodies are supposed to look. They show us these models who are 5'11" and weigh 110 pounds. That is so not your average American woman. I read a funny article in the *Chicago Sun-Times* recently that said the average American woman 10 years ago weighed 140 pounds. Today she weighs 152. Sixty years ago, the average American bottom was 14 inches across. Today it's two inches wider. Which is too bad, because the width of the average toilet seat is only 14 and a half inches. The average dress size for an American woman is between 12 and 14. So why are they only showing skinny women on magazines and TV?

🌀 We all have our set point when it comes to weight. If you're meant to weigh 135 pounds, chances are that's the zone you're going to wind up in, no matter how much you diet. Genetics is pretty ruthless that way. But that doesn't mean you shouldn't be a really fit and toned 135 pounds. Even if you're built large or stocky, you can still have a strong, healthy, and attractive body.

🌀 My mother's always been on me to lose weight, watching every bite of food that I swallow. She got me to go to this workshop on body image, and I was feeling like, give me a break, will you? But it turned out to be pretty interesting. They did this one thing where they asked us to write down the names of three people in history we most admired. Well, people wrote down Martin Luther King, Eleanor Roosevelt, Gandhi, Jesus, Mother Teresa. Nobody wrote down Kate Moss or Courtney Cox or anybody like that just because they were skinny. In fact, the skinniest person on the list was probably Abraham Lincoln.

Fitting in Fitness

Eating wisely is one way to keep your weight under control; exercising is another. When you put the two together, you have this physical and chemical reaction, and before you know it, the pounds start to melt. Exercise is not only vital for weight control, but it also helps us to think more clearly, combat stress, and ward off depression. Factoring exercise into your busy life can be a challenge, however. Some ideas from fellow restaurant professionals on the subject follow:

🕮 Most important piece of advice: don't make the training so hard that you get discouraged. Some people go out there and they want to be Iron Men and Iron Women right at the start. Doesn't happen that way. Give yourself a chance.

✪ Three to five exercise sessions a week is all you really have to do, anywhere from a half-hour to an hour per session.

✪ I only do exercise that I think is fun. If I'm bored, I'm not going to stay with it. So at first I did a lot of aerobic dancing, which I love, and then recently I added swimming, to mix things up.

✪ Some people just assume that to get fit you're going to have to join some fancy gym, and you're going to walk in there, with your little pot belly and the hair on your shoulders, and you're going to feel lower than low, so why bother anyway? To those people, I say, you don't have to join a health club to get exercise. Walk up steps instead of using the elevator. Walk to work if it's at all possible. If you go to the mall, instead of circling for 20 minutes looking for a parking spot that's close to the stores, park really far away, and use those 20 minutes to get a good walk in. When you develop that kind of thinking, you'll find fitness opportunities all over the place.

✪ I like exercising with a friend. An exercise buddy, if you will. Someone to support me, encourage me, and keep me company. Is that so much to ask?

✪ Train, don't strain. If something hurts, pay attention. If you're breathing too hard to be able to carry on a conversation, stop. And, seriously, check with your physician before starting any kind of exercise program. I know you've heard that before, but it makes sense.

Some Well-Earned Rest

You can be as fit as a fiddle, you can eat the most nutritious food, you can get regular checkups, and you can avoid tobacco and alcohol, but if you don't get your sleep, then you're not going to be a well person. Sleep is critical to your health. Scientists don't really know why humans need to sleep; all they know is that it's entirely necessary. Some researchers theorize that the purpose of sleep is to reduce certain chemicals that have built up in the body during the waking hours. Beyond that, sleep is a blessed refuge from the stress and overstimulation epidemic in our society. Unfortunately, however, a great many of us have difficulty achieving the kind of sleep we'd like to enjoy.

What are the effects of insufficient sleep? The answer is serious, indeed. Research shows that after as few as six days of reduced sleep—anything less than four hours a night—can limit the body's ability to metabolize carbohydrates. And what does that mean? Well, for one thing, if you're sleeping less and eating more junk food—which you're apt to do if you're stressed from sleeping less—then you have less chance to metabolize all those corn chips, potato chips, burritos, and whatnot and more of a chance of developing a weight problem. Sleep deprivation also can lead to accidents. According to the National Highway Traffic Safety Administration, over 100,000 automobile accidents occur each year because of sleep-deprived drivers.

In fact, research shows that driving while sleepy is as dangerous as driving while intoxicated. If you still believe that sleep deprivation is not such a big deal, then think about the research experiment that exposed laboratory rats to increasingly diminished sleep. As a result of this sleep deprivation, the rats died within two to four weeks. Now *that's* serious!

So what constitutes an adequate amount of sleep? It varies from person to person. Most people sleep in one long expanse of six to eight hours. Some of us are more inclined to sleep for five or six hours at a stretch and maybe have a nap, no more than an hour, in the afternoon. Think about your own sleep habits. Is falling asleep hard for you? Do you tend to wake up a lot? Do you feel tired during the day? If so, you're not alone. Let's hear what fellow restaurant professionals have to say, for this is an industry where sleep deprivation can become a real problem.

The best advice I know of with regard to sleeping is to keep to a regular schedule. Your system really resents those nights when you only get two or three hours of sleep, and sleeping in the afternoon won't make up the deficit.

Caffeine is a real sleep-buster. I never touch the stuff after four in the afternoon. Be smart and steer clear of spicy foods late at night too. I know that when you're working in the restaurant business, it's easy to just grab some pulled pork or chili or whatever's around before you go home, but that stuff can keep you up at night. Exercising late at night is another bad idea. Don't expect to get your body all riled up with a workout and then fall into bed and float off to sleep. It doesn't happen that way.

🌜 It may sound like common sense, but try to relax before you get into bed. And even though watching TV may *seem* relaxing, you'll be better off experimenting with activities that don't involve being electronically stimulated. Have a warm bath instead, and get into bed with a good—or, better yet, boring—book.

🌜 Music is such a help in getting to sleep. I particularly love all that Celtic New Age stuff. It's better than anything that comes in a bottle.

🌜 Any kind of extremes in room temperature can cost me a night's sleep. Too warm, too cold . . . forget about it.

🌜 Noise is a big issue for me. I live upstairs from a bar, and there's noise all night long, so I use a "white noise" machine that plays sounds of nature, like waterfalls and ocean surf. If that doesn't work, I use earplugs. There are some excellent, super-pliable earplugs on the market these days.

🌜 Here's something to keep in mind: if you have trouble sleeping, don't turn on the lights to read or watch TV. It's better to try to stay with your normal light-dark schedule and just remain in the dark, listening to music if you want.

🌜 A lot of people are big on naps, and even 15 or 20 minutes of shut-eye can go a long way, but remember that keeping on schedule is key when it comes to establishing good sleep patterns. So if you nap, schedule your naps so you're having them at roughly the same time every day.

✆ When all else fails, I've used sleeping pills, and they work for me. But you should never be on them unless you're under the care of a doctor, and in any case, you shouldn't be on them for more than four weeks at a time.

Bad Habits

Now that we've examined some ways that can lead you toward wellness, such as good eating, sleeping, and fitness, let's spend a few minutes considering some of the self-destructive behaviors with which people get involved. The worst is probably substance abuse, which includes both drinking and drug use (these often go hand in hand, by the way) and smoking. The figures on American lives lost to these bad habits every year are truly sobering, if not downright overwhelming.

The wide availability of alcoholic beverages can be a particular problem for those working in the restaurant field. Being surrounded by fine wines and beer and other liquors can turn a habit of drinking in moderation into a habit of drinking to excess, particularly when alcohol is being used to relieve stress. Now's the time to start thinking about your relationship to such substances. A good way to begin is to listen to what your colleagues have to say.

🎧 I'm a wine steward, and I have to admit that when it came to drinking, I really wasn't watching myself. Being surrounded by these great wines all the time, I started to drink more than I should. I guess I deluded myself into thinking I was only drinking for professional purposes, when, in fact, I was drinking when I was stressed, just like other people do.

🎧 All you have to do is hang around restaurants for a few weeks, and you can see, firsthand, how many people have drinking problems. I'm talking about customers, and I'm talking about staff. As a bartender, I'm often in the situation where I have to tell somebody, "Enough," and that's the least favorite part of my job.

🎧 I have customers who drink hard liquor all through dinner, and it's a shame because they're not even tasting the incredible food we serve.

🎧 I've been a waiter for over 20 years, and I can remember the days when people put their cigarettes out in the mashed potatoes. All I can sat is "Hallelujah" now that there's no smoking in restaurants in New York. I love it!

🎧 The biggest joke is low-tar cigarettes. Don't people realize that those just make you smoke more and harder?

🎧 Stopping smoking was a real challenge for me. Tobacco is so powerfully addictive. You've got to find what works for you, and that may require experimentation. Whether it's gum or patches or hypnosis or [an American] Cancer Society program—it's up to you to find out. Just do it!

❨❨ To stop smoking, first you need the motivation. Then you need help. Where do you get the help? Start with your doctor or dentist. If that's not convenient, check out the Web sites of organizations like the American Lung Association (http://www.lungusa.org), the American Heart Association (http://www. americanheart.org), or the American Cancer Society (http://www.cancer.org).

The Comfort Zone

While we're on the subject of taking care of yourself, let's not forget some important ways to protect and relieve your aching body. After all, the restaurant business can take a heavy toll on your body. Keep the following tips from your colleagues in mind:

❨❨ A good pair of shoes makes all the difference. You'll want a lot of arch support to preserve your strength and energy. Forget about sneakers.

❨❨ If you're on your feet all day long, then you have to treat them right when you get home. Maybe you'll want to soak your feet in some Epsom salts or give them a massage after showering. Dry them thoroughly, especially between the toes, and put on a little antiseptic foot lotion or natural foot powder afterwards. I've found that seeing a podiatrist at regular intervals can make a big difference too.

💿 Every now and then, when I'm on the job, I find that I get really exhausted. If this happens to you, try this. Find someplace where you can lie down on your back, just for five minutes, with your head resting on a rolled-up towel and your feet up on a chair. People may make fun of you, but who cares? It's a lifesaver.

Stressed Out

As a restaurant professional, you're in a performance field, which means you probably feel a good deal of pressure or even stress a lot of the time. You're not in a low-stress profession where no one's watching you. You're out there, in the world, playing your part in what can be a very complicated operation, and that can make you nervous. What's more, you're living in a stressful time in history.

Of course, it could be argued that all eras of history have their significant stressors, and that's true. The Black Plague, the Crusades, the Civil War, the Great Depression, Pearl Harbor . . . whew! Historians could even argue that we have less stress in our lives now than our ancestors did. After all, we have more leisure time due to increased technology and better medical care, to name just two stress-relieving factors. But we also have rapidly developing problems with overpopulation and pollution, and we live with the horrifying knowledge that a push of a button could destroy cities and even civilizations. Therefore, many people in the world today experience life as being *increasingly* stressful.

In addition to stress at work and in the world at large are the stresses an individual must confront in his or her own life. A death in the family, marital discord, financial reversals, and illness or injury can rapidly up the ante on stress. So the question becomes, what can you do to alleviate all of this unhealthy stress? Keep in mind how important that relief is, for if stress goes untreated, it can cause physical complications such as high blood pressure, headaches, gastritis and acid reflux, and more. Let's hear how fellow restaurant professionals confront and combat stress.

The more flexible you are, the less stress you'll feel. I've always been something of a control freak—this field is full of people like me—but I'm learning how to go with the flow. It isn't easy—as I said, it goes against my basic nature—but my job and my marriage could be at stake if I can't learn to lighten up a little.

My solution to my stress problem was to basically give up on the idea of perfection. I have a demanding job as a banquet manager; I have two kids and a husband at home; and I've always prided myself on being able to keep my balls up in the air. But the fact is that all of that juggling has been taking its toll, and recently I began to get terrible stress headaches—you know, the kind where you feel like there's a steel band tightening around your skull? I've finally come to the realization that I need to let certain things go. I have to learn to accept unmade beds and takeout pizza for dinner. Once I do that, I think I'll begin to feel some relief.

💿 There *is* a magic bullet when it comes to curing stress. It's learning how to say "no." N-O. That's the most important word in the English language, and one of the hardest to say. Once you get good at saying it, you'll see how much stress you can slough off. "No, I'm sorry, I can't. It's my son's graduation." "No, I'm sorry, but that won't work out. I have a doctor's appointment." "No, sorry, but I'm already doing so much extra work as it is." Without that word "no," the stuff just keeps piling on, and your stress reading goes off the charts.

💿 The nature of stress is that it's explosive, it's invasive, and you can quickly get carried away by it. Stress in one area can have you thinking, "Oh, my Lord. I've made a complete mess of things. I've screwed up bigtime. I'm a complete flop." What you have to do is step back one or two giant steps and tell yourself, "I'm having a problem in one area of my life right now, but elsewhere I'm in good shape. Everything's good on the family front, my health is good, my house is good, my car is good, yadda yadda." Don't let yourself get carried away on the tidal wave of stress.

💿 Make sure that you treat stress as a medical problem. Why? Because it is. Talk to your physician, and get a stress management plan in place. The longer stress goes untreated, the more damage it can do.

Stress Relief

So what can you do to make yourself feel better when you're under a lot of stress? Some practical, everyday ways of dealing with stress, courtesy of your colleagues, follow:

💿 Deep breathing is the place to begin. It's free, it's easy, and anyone can do it anywhere, anytime. Start by inhaling deeply through your nose, filling up your lungs. Then hold that breath while you count to six. Don't just let it out all at once, but exhale slowly, counting once more to six. Then repeat, and continue to do this for several minutes. You'll start feeling better in no time.

💿 You can boost the value of deep breathing by chanting to yourself "in with the good" on the inhalations and "out with the bad" on the exhalations. It's a simple way to rid your mind of toxins.

💿 Communication is really great anti-stress therapy. Sometimes all it takes is a word or two from somebody nearby to get you back on the straight and narrow. Get yourself a confidante. Someone you can really trust. Maybe it's your sister, maybe it's your aunt, maybe it's your priest, maybe it's your family doctor . . . who knows? You know. Just pick someone out and confide in that person, and you'll feel the burden lifting.

🕮 Developing your spiritual side can be really helpful in dealing with stress. I didn't grow up with any religion, but I started going to this church with a great gospel choir right here in my neighborhood, and when I sit there on a Sunday, I feel like a whole other person.

🕮 This may seem obvious, but if you're feeling exhausted and worn down by stress, it may be time to see a mental health professional. If you have a bad tooth, you'd go to a dentist, right? If you have bunions, you'd see a podiatrist. Same thing here. You're in need of help, and there's plenty of help out there. It doesn't have to be a long-term commitment either. Sometimes a short intervention of five or six sessions can clear up whatever's bothering you.

🕮 Communication with people is important, but who says you can't communicate with your dog or cat or bird in a way that makes you feel better?

🕮 For me, the best way to keep stress under control is regular exercise. When those endorphins break free, you'll feel far away from your stress, believe me.

🕮 The best antidote I've found for stress is a good laugh. It'll clear out your system. I watch a really hilarious video, like *Tootsie* or *A Fish Called Wanda* or *I Love Lucy*. I mean, when Lucy's doing that Vitametavegamin commercial, and you're laughing yourself silly, how can stress stand a chance?

🕮 A friend of mine gave me a present of Loretta La Roche tapes for the car. She's this advocate of laughter as therapy, and she's very funny and very real. You can check out her Web site at <http://www.stressed.com>.

🕮 My greatest stress reliever is working in my wood-shop. When I'm building a birdhouse, I am feeling no pain. You wouldn't believe how many birdhouses I've made!

🕮 Uh, excuse me, but have you tried a vacation? A week away is a great help. Two weeks can be a cure-all. Americans don't take nearly enough vacation. In Europe, everybody takes at least a month off in the summer. Here we're crazy workaholics, and stress is regarded as a normal, if not a positive, thing. I don't buy into that.

🕮 Who says a vacation has to cost money? To me, a vacation is anything that breaks the pattern and the cycle that's causing you stress. Take a few days off, stay home, paint the foyer, go for a ferry boat [ride] across the river, or for a picnic in the park, or go to the beach, and you'll see how much better you feel.

The issues we've discussed in this chapter are very important, but a big factor in your health is the environment in which you work. We discuss this in the next chapter.

Chapter Reference

Sleep deprivation statistics accessed March 2004 at, http://my.webmd.com/content/article/64/72426.htm

Chapter 6

Better Safe Than Sorry

hink back to the days before you went into the restaurant business, when you were a consumer rather than a provider. Chances are, you'd go out for a meal without giving any real thought to the dangers that might befall you. You didn't think about microbes and foreign objects in the food and fires and accidents. You just ordered your meat loaf and mashed potatoes and went on you merry way, isn't that so?

But now you're an insider, and you understand the seriousness of safety and sanitation within a restaurant setting. Now you recognize that when you invite people into your restaurant, you are literally taking their lives into your hands. Outbreaks of salmonella or E. coli can kill people. Did you know that there was once an outbreak of food poisoning in Sweden that affected over *8,000 people!* Tragically, 90 died. Foreign objects in food, such as pits, shells, or, heaven forbid, broken glass, also can injure people or even cause death. Obviously and fortunately, there are many more people who survive eating in restaurants than those who expire from the experience. But even so, ask yourself how you would feel if a tragedy came about as a result of your negligence.

Restaurants present dangers to those who work in them as well. There is always the potential for accidents, with people running into each other carrying heavy trays or burning themselves on hot pots. When you combine close quarters with heat, heavy objects, sharp objects, and a lot of running around, you have the potential for problems. This chapter is all about safeguarding against these problems. So let us begin.

Hygiene and Sanitation

According to the U.S. Public Health Service, there are more than 40 diseases that are food-transferable. That means you should be careful about where you eat. As far as we're concerned, we'd choose a spanking clean diner any day over a four-star restaurant that takes shortcuts when it comes to hygiene and sanitation. Food-borne illnesses such as hepatitis and salmonella are the sorts of things you wouldn't wish on your worst enemy, but they can be largely prevented with good sanitation practices. Hygiene and sanitation begin with *you*. Let's look at the section that follows to see how you're measuring up.

Personal Hygiene

Did you ever hear of Typhoid Mary? Her given name was Mary Mallon, and she was the first person found to be a "healthy carrier" of typhoid fever in the United States. That means that she had no outward signs of illness, but she could infect others. And infect others she did. In 1906, she went to work as a cook for a wealthy New York City family that was spending the summer on Long Island. Every member of the family came down with typhoid fever, and eventually the out-break and the subsequent deaths of 47 people were traced back to Mallon. Her name went down in infamy. You wouldn't want that to happen to your good name, would you?

One way to safeguard your good name is to begin with good hygiene. Your fellow professionals offer some advice.

☙ A clean uniform is not just more attractive, but it's also much safer. Scrupulous laundering of your uniform will help keep the microbes at bay.

☙ Buy each component of your uniform in multiples of two or three—whatever you can afford. That way you can dress in clean items every day without having to do laundry every day.

Laundry List of Stain Removers

Your uniform is one way you present yourself to your clientele, and it may also represent a significant investment, thus it's important to know how to maintain it and keep it free from stains. The "Top 10" stains, along with the proper procedure for their removal, follow:

1. **Wine.** Stretch material over a bowl, and pour boiling water through.

2. **Berries.** Sponge with lemon juice, flush with water, and allow to dry.

3. **Blood.** Soak as soon as possible in salted water. Wash in cold water.

4. **Butter.** Gentle scrape away residue, then dampen the stain and rub in powdered detergent. A dry cleaning fluid may be necessary.

5. **Chocolate.** Remove excess chocolate with a scraper, and then sponge with cold water or soak for 30 minutes in an enzyme prewash solution. Rub detergent into the stain, and then flush with cold water. A final treatment with a dry cleaning fluid may be necessary.

6. **Coffee and tea.** Blot, and then rinse with cool water. Rub in detergent, and proceed with machine washing.

7. **Egg.** Scrape off solid matter, and then soak in a nonmetal container with an enzyme solution for up to eight hours. Make sure

your stain is out before you dry your item, for drying will set the stain.

8. **Oil.** Olive, canola, safflower . . . you name it. Scrub with distilled water and soap.

9. **Meat juices.** Sponge with cold water, and wash in cold water.

10. **Tomato sauce.** Sprinkle the stain with powdered dishwasher detergent, and rub it in with a toothbrush. Proceed with your laundering, and if the stain lingers, dry the item in the sun to bleach out the stain residue.

📞 Good grooming is a general must. Keep your nails trimmed. Overly long nails trap all kinds of bacteria. If you have a beard, keep it trimmed. And, by the way, don't use perfumes or aftershave if you're serving food. The odors get in the way of the wonderful food odors.

📞 Obviously, if you have any cuts or open sores, you'll have to make sure you deal with them according to the first-aid policy of your workplace.

📞 You know the sign in the bathroom that tells you to wash your hands? It's serious. Very, very serious.

📞 Remember those times when you've gone to the dentist and the hygienist gave you this special rinse to swish around in your mouth? All the parts you missed came out blue, right? Well, the same sort of product exists that you can use when you do your sanitation and hygiene training for your staff. It's a special powder that you put on your hands. After you've washed, look at your hands in infrared light, and see all the places where the powder glows that didn't come clean.

✒ I've worked in restaurants that require a regular physical examination for employees. I think this is a highly commendable idea. Short of that, a lot of restaurants require physical examinations for incoming employees, which is absolutely critical, I think, particularly when you're hiring people from developing countries that have high rates of illnesses like hepatitis and tuberculosis. An incoming examination will also protect your establishment against any disability claims where the employee says the disability was incurred on the job, and you know very well it wasn't.

✒ Keep in mind that, as a manager or assistant manager, it is your job to look at people critically. Certain shortcomings—soiled uniforms, body odor, dirty hands, scratching, sneezing—are not just unattractive but can also suggest the existence of or the possibility for infection. Don't be shy at getting to the root of the problem.

Wash Those Hands

Medical science made a great breakthrough hundreds of years ago when some smart doctors figured out that there was a connection between the conscientious washing of hands by medical personnel and the reduced mortality rates among patients.

The same precautions apply to restaurant professionals, who need to learn the proper techniques for hand washing.

When to Do It:

Always take a few moments to wash your hands in the following situations:

- before starting work

- after using the lavatory

- after handling raw food

- after touching your hair, coughing, sneezing, blowing your nose, or touching any type of waste or refuse

- often during the day, as it occurs to you. You cannot *overwash* your hands!

How to Do It:

Follow these steps and you'll be doing it right:

- rinse hands

- wash thoroughly with approved soap

- rub soap through fingers, thumbs, and all over palms

- rinse thoroughly

- use paper towel or hot air dryer to dry hands

- turn off tap with paper towel

Safe Food Handling

Okay, okay—we know we've said it before, but we'll say it again, because this is one of those things you can't say too many times: inadequate sanitation and improper food handling can cause sickness and death. It can also cause the death of your establishment. Nothing will end a restaurant's life quite so quickly as a serious outbreak of food poisoning. Your colleagues comment on the topic.

📣 I never, never eat in a restaurant that doesn't look clean. Do you think I'm crazy? You want a laundry list of serious diseases that you can get from eating in a dirty restaurant? Let's see. Well, there's salmonella, of course. Then there's hepatitis, typhoid, diphtheria . . . whoa, I'm scaring myself. Now you're going to say, come on, does this kind of thing happen often? The answer is "often enough." Which is too often for me.

📣 Is it possible for spoiled food to make its way out of the kitchen? Yes, my friends, it is. Having managed a restaurant for almost 10 years, I can tell you that we've had instances where a server has picked up on the fact that something has an off-smell, even though our cooks didn't. Incredible? Well, in one case, the cook was recovering from a head cold that had affected his sense of smell. In another case, we had an idiot cook. What can I say? As a server, keep your eyes and your nose open, because you've got to be the gatekeeper too. What we don't want is any spoiled food to get to the customer!

📣 Stay far away from the contents of any cans that are rusty, corroded, or that bulge suspiciously. Ever hear of botulism? And the tops of cans should always be washed off before you open them. That way if there are any vermin droppings, heaven forbid, they won't get into the food.

✺ Food storage is a very important issue. Some foods do not keep well. Dishes like aspics, for instance, that you might have on a buffet table are made with agar-agar, the very raw material that's used in the lab to grow cultures! Unless you're planning to do an interesting science experiment, dispose of any aspic left over on the buffet table, and chalk it up to waste.

✺ Part of your job as a restaurant manager is to always be on the outlook for problems and to head them off at the pass before they cause any trouble. So train yourself to have a roving eye. Give the kitchen the once-over on a regular basis, even a daily basis, and see what needs work or what needs to be changed altogether. Look at the counters. Are they constructed of materials like marble or stainless steel that cannot be penetrated by any substances that could harbor bacteria? They should be. What about your waste disposal system? The garbage cans need to be cleaned on a regular basis too, inside and out.

✺ Very important when you're managing a restaurant: make sure that there's a dishwashing regimen in place, and that everyone signs on to it. It should go like this: (1) preclean with a little scrubbing and scraping; (2) clean top to bottom with detergent; (3) rinse thoroughly; (4) zap any remaining bacteria with a sanitizer; (5) rinse again; (6) allow dishes to air-dry.

🌀 There need to be separate towels for the hands and for the dishes.

The "V" Word

That's "V" for "vermin" . . . and nothing will close down a kitchen faster than if a health inspector sees signs of "critters." Everyone who works in a restaurant should have their antennae up—excuse the expression—for telltale signs that unwanted visitors are lurking. These include:

🌀 *Droppings.* No, ladies and gentlemen, those are not poppy seeds. The small, dry variety are mouse droppings. The leave-behinds of rats—shudder—are naturally larger and are moist when fresh.

🌀 *Damage.* The way birds fly, rodents gnaw . . . through just about anything. If you see signs of their favorite activity—on foods, but also on wood, soap, or even pipes—you'll know you're not alone.

🌀 *Smears.* Ugh, ugh, and double-ugh. These "ugh-ly" marks occur when the greasy, dirty fur of rodents comes into contact with kitchen surfaces.

🌀 *Disappearance of bait.* Here today and gone tomorrow can only mean one thing: There's a mouse (or worse) in the house.

What to do if you see any of the above? Try the following: (1) Remove any hiding places, such as cartons, crates, or other forms of rubbish. (2) Fill rat holes with steel wool, concrete mixed with glass, or other such impenetrable materials. (3) Store all food in rodent-proof containers. And most important of all—call the exterminator! If a rat runs across your dining room while customers are there, you can kiss your business good-bye.

I think I'd rather see a mouse than cockroaches. Oooh, how I hate those ugly bugs. They're ugly, they're dirty, they're smelly, and they carry bacteria like shigella and salmonella. In truth, they don't spread disease nearly as much as houseflies will, but they're just horrible.

If you want to get the most out of a disinfectant, make it nice and hot. Cold disinfectant doesn't hold a candle to hot disinfectant.

As a manager, I have to keep in mind, first and foremost, that good hygiene and sanitation in the kitchen is very much an issue of continuing education—for me as well as for the people who work under me. I have to stay informed about any new dangers out there and any new ways of dealing with these dangers. All of us have to work toward the same goal, and the best way to do that is by holding regular training sessions, using visual aids like posters, giving out awards and prizes for those who meet the goals we've set, and that kind of thing.

Cleaning Tips

Two of the most important things to keep in mind when cleaning are to make sure that the job that's done is thorough and that cleaning occurs on a regular schedule. That means certain aspects of your restaurant's cleaning will be done on a daily, weekly, and biweekly basis, and so forth. Let's listen to what your fellow restaurant professionals have to say about staying spic and span:

✆ Change your sponges often, and in between changes, disinfect them. What's the best way to disinfect a sponge? Not by running it through the dishwasher, as some people say. It may be easy, but it doesn't kill off all the bacteria. Some people nuke their sponges in the microwave, but if you're not careful, you can burn the sponge or set off sparks if impurities are imbedded in the sponge. Try this instead: boil the sponge on the stovetop for five minutes. That'll be the death knell for any bacteria that happens to be present.

✆ Some of us may choose to deny it, but can openers can get really grungy. I clean them by running a sheet of paper towel through them.

✆ Everybody has their own methods of cleaning pots and pans. I've found that the best and easiest way to do this is to fill the pan with salted water and set it over high heat until the water boils. As the temperature of the water increases, the gunk will loosen, and you can scrape it free with a wooden spoon.

🕮 Spilled oil can be really treacherous. Clean up the spill by sprinkling a layer of flour over the oil. Within a few minutes, the flour should have absorbed the oil. Use a paper towel (or a brush if you suspect that broken glass might be present) to move the flour around, making sure that all the oil gets absorbed, and then sweep the whole business into a dustpan. You can finish up by spraying the area with a glass cleaner.

Food Handling

As a restaurant professional, you have to be aware of what happens to food when it sits out and sits around. Very bad things can happen to it, in fact. Some tips from fellow restaurant professionals follow about taking care of the food served in your establishment:

🕮 Pick up a magazine these days and you'll find yourself reading about the "wonderful flavors that emerge when food [is] served at room temperature." This is particularly true of those trendy Mediterranean *cucina fresca* preparations you see all over the place these days. In fact, a great deal of flavor does emerge at this temperature, but it's also the ideal temperature to encourage the development of bacteria and pathogens that can do so much damage. You'll really be a lot better off keeping your extra quantities warm on a range, in the oven, or in some other kind of warmer. Or, if applicable, keep it all cold, in the fridge.

📞 In our restaurant, rare meats are a thing of the past. We're not taking any chances, thank-you very much. One outbreak of E. coli and we might as well pick up our jacks and go home. If you have any kind of involvement with a restaurant at all, keep yourself informed about any new guidelines with regard to the suggested internal temperatures for meat, fish, poultry, and so forth.

📞 It's unbelievable how costly an outbreak of food-borne illness can be. Ten years ago, a two-year-old ate a cheeseburger at a Jack-in-the-Box in Washington State. Ten days later, he died of E. coli. Almost 500 people got sick from the same shipment of meat. Not only was the cost staggering in terms of human pain and suffering, but the company's stock plunged from nearly $14 a share to less than $9. Sales dropped overall about 30 percent, and a whole bunch of lawsuits were filed against the company. What's more, millions of potential customers would never step foot near a Jack-in-the-Box again. It's a classic story of its type, and it drives home the point we've all been talking about here—that you're dealing with people's *lives*.

📞 We all know that if we visit developing countries, we don't drink the water, and we pay close attention to what we eat. In the United States, fortunately, we have a lot of inspection and a lot of supervision of what is served in restaurants. But I really wish we could do even better here. In Japan, it's common for people to wear a surgical mask if they have a cold. There's no stigma to it; that's just the way it's done. Think of how much sickness we could head off at the pass if we did that sort of thing here.

☙ Is your refrigerator cold enough? I remember hearing about a restaurant where an outbreak of staph occurred because the coconut custard pies were stored in a refrigerator at a temperature between 52° and 60°.

☙ When I came into the restaurant where I'm working now, we were doing a buffet lunch, and I saw one of the staff refilling a serving dish that had held a crab-meat salad. I almost jumped out of my skin. The residue of the salad had already been sitting out for a period of time. From that point on, we instituted a policy that when a serving dish is empty on a buffet table, you must always clean it out before adding more food. Better yet, start with a fresh dish altogether. Better safe than sorry.

☙ Buffets can be like landmines—so dangerous. So many people picking up tongs and serving spoons or putting their hands into serving bowls to pick out an olive or whatever. It's a real field day for cross-contamination. All the serving spoons and tongs and ladles— they all have to be cleaned and sanitized every half hour. Or, better yet, replace them with fresh ones.

The "Top 10" Rules of Bacteria Control

Bacteria are living organisms, thus they require food, moisture, the proper pH, and time to grow. They particularly love foods that are high in protein, such as dairy and meat, and they *really* love eggs, fish, and shellfish. They also can't resist mayonnaise, hollandaise sauce, custards, and other egg-filled treats.

Our "Top 10" tips on how to control bacteria follow:

1. Heat internal temperatures to 140°.

2. When holding food, make sure you maintain that 140° internal temperature.

3. Only heat small quantities at a time. When you heat large quantities, it is difficult to maintain the consistency of the temperature throughout.

4. Heat foods rapidly.

5. Heat foods close to the time you'll be serving them.

6. Never use a steam table to reheat foods. Heat them rapidly to the internal temperature recommended above, and then transfer to the steam table.

7. To chill hot foods quickly, put them in an ice bath or under cold running water.

8. When placing cooked foods in the refrigerator, always place them above uncooked food. This will prevent cross-contamination.

9. *Never* thaw foods at room temperature. Thaw them in the refrigerator in a container so they don't drip their contents onto other foods.

10. Use your head!

Special Tips for Servers

Servers have the most contact with the food after the cooks and before the customer. Some tips especially for servers follow:

📢 Always handle glassware by the stems or the bottoms, never by the rims.

📢 Hold dishes away from the bottom, not by hooking your thumbs over the top surface.

📢 Never stack dishes or glassware when serving.

📢 Obvious, but it must be said: Handle flatware and utensils *by the handles*, not by the cutting or serving surfaces.

📢 You wouldn't ever touch food with your bare hands, would you?

📢 Use plastic or metal tongs or scoops for ice. Never use your hands, and never dip glassware into the ice.

📢 Cloths used for food spills or on eating surfaces do not get used anywhere else, understand?

Interfacing with Your Inspector

Part of being in the restaurant business is the periodic visit from the health inspector. In terms of the anxiety this can generate, it is right up there with a visit from a restaurant critic. Think positively, however. In building a satisfying relationship with your local health inspector, you can greatly benefit your operation and even find ways to avoid making costly mistakes. Remember, you and the inspector are on the same side: you both want to keep the customer from getting sick!

Since you both have the same goal, you can best reach that goal by establishing a basis of trust and a good line of communication. Some tips from fellow restaurant professionals follow that will cue you in on how this is done:

📖 First of all, don't take anything personally. Leave your paranoia at home that day. The inspector is just doing his job. And if he finds problems, be grateful. The small problems he finds today may keep you from making disastrous mistakes in the future.

📖 Be polite and professional, as you would with anyone. Don't be surprised if the inspector turns up at a mealtime. Even though it may be inconvenient for you to have her around then, she has chosen that time expressly to see how you prepare food.

📖 Don't be afraid to ask questions. Regard this as a learning experience all around.

〰〰〰〰 Join the inspector on the tour. Seeing the way he works will help you understand how you need to think in between his visits. Bring a note pad with you, and jot down any observations as you go along. That will show how seriously you're taking this. And believe me—it *is* serious.

〰〰〰〰 Don't go running after the inspector with éclairs or bruschetta. You're not going to change her mind about anything by "bribing" her with tidbits, no matter how delicious they may be. All you'll wind up doing is looking like you're trying to bribe her . . . and how good is that?

〰〰〰〰 Don't go into road rage, ever. No matter how much you might disagree with what he says or does, keep it to yourself. You can respond to his report by letter. You certainly don't ever want to get into a screaming match with your health inspector.

Watch Your Back . . . Watch Your Front

Let us say it once again: Restaurants can be dangerous places, with knives, hot surfaces, slippery floors, heavy items to lift, and people to bump—or crash—into. Some tips from restaurant professionals that will help protect you follow:

〰〰〰〰 As a manager, it is your duty to protect your customers and to protect your staff. That means that you— that's right, *you*—are responsible for making sure that your restaurant has a safety policy in place. It has to be one that is thought out *and* written out, so that everyone can sign onto it. In other words, easy words and bilingual, if your situation calls for it. This document should include the names of the staff members who have been made responsible for fire safety and prevention, for personal injuries, for Occupational Safety and Health Administration (OSHA) compliance, for first aid, and for safety training. If you don't already have something like this in place, what are you waiting for?

❧ You can have the best safety policies in place, but if morale is poor in your shop, then you can expect accidents. It's true—accidents occur when people are feeling stressed, and people feel stressed if the environment is rife with infighting and backbiting and indifference. Such places tend to be dangerous places, not just emotionally or psychologically but physically too.

❧ As a manager, pay close attention to scheduling, and make sure that people are taking their breaks. Tired people are people who have accidents . . . or who *cause* accidents.

❧ Training is key. You've got dangerous equipment around: knives and slicing machines and all kinds of stuff. People who are starting out and haven't been trained adequately, or people who have been doing the same job for so long that they're on automatic pilot are the ones who have the accidents.

❧ Never scrimp on safety. Better you should use a leaner piece of meat than cut back on your lighting. Better you should buy a less expensive brand of ice cream than subject your staff to poor ventilation. When conditions are not what they should be—poor lighting, poor ventilation, too little or too much heat—that's when accidents occur.

🌀 Part of the manager's job is to survey the restaurant on a regular basis and to make sure that the physical plant is in good repair. Broken tiles, curling-up carpet, faulty plumbing—these will all cause accidents or illness. Don't allow that to happen.

🌀 Your staff can open themselves up to injury if they're dressed inappropriately for their work. No one in the front of the house or the back of the house should be wearing ribbons or jewelry dangling from their ears or their wrists or wherever. These things can get caught, and serious injuries can occur. Leave the geegaws at home.

🌀 Clutter control goes a long way toward preventing accidents. Everyone should be indoctrinated in the principle of *mise en place*—everthing in its place. When you use something, you put it back where it belongs when you're finished.

🌀 Open drawers? Ouch.

🌀 Pot handles turned to the rear, of course.

🌀 Store heavy items on low shelves. If you're taking a heavy pot down from a high shelf, it could slip out of your hands, fall on your head, and cause major head trauma.

🌀 Here's an accident that's waiting to happen: trying to slice frozen food. That's just plain crazy. Wait for the food to thaw, and *then* slice it.

🌀 We're not kids anymore. When we fall, we get more than a boo-boo. We get broken bones, head injuries, back injuries. So make sure that everyone on your staff is on the same page regarding the prevention of falls. Shoes need to be tied, long skirts that you can trip over need to be left at home, and spills need to be wiped up the second they happen.

🌀 I've witnessed so-called restaurant "professionals" reaching for something up high on a chair with telephone books piled up under their feet. Great way to get yourself killed. Use real step stools, for heaven's sake. That's what they're made for.

🌀 Walk, don't run. Make that the foundation of all your safety training. Put it up on the walls, stamp it on people's pay envelopes, tattoo it on foreheads.

🌀 I remember seeing silent-movie comedies where the waiter's got this tray piled up with dishes way high and he can't see where he's going and he's sort of bobbing and weaving around the joint. That's funny, but life's not a silent-movie comedy. In real life, if you can't see where you're going, you can cause an accident that can result in serious injury to yourself or someone else. Hardy-har-har.

🌀 If you've got a double-door arrangement somewhere in your restaurant, make sure that the doors are marked IN and OUT, and make sure that everybody knows which is which.

🌀 Give a good look-around to your restaurant. See any overhangs or places where people could hit their heads? If it's not removable—if, for instance, it's a permanent support beam—then you'll want to outline the overhang with some kind of brightly colored tape or some other eye-catching device.

Slash 'n Burn

Knives, fires, toxic chemicals . . . there are a lot of ways to get hurt in a restaurant. Here's how our restaurant professionals safeguard themselves:

What's safer—a sharp knife or a dull knife? No, that wasn't a trick question—the correct answer is a sharp knife. Dull knives make you work harder and apply more pressure. The harder you work, and the more frustration you experience over poor results, the more likely you are to slip.

Promise that you'll never, ever, hold an item in your hand when you're cutting it. All cutting should be done on a cutting board or other hard surface. Believe it or not, I've seen people cut a potato holding it in their hands. Now that may look good in those old Western movies, but please—not in real life.

Never cut with the knife blade facing your body, and always make sure that your hands are dry when using a knife.

Always carry knives point down.

Don't try to catch a falling knife. You're not a circus performer.

✺ There's a right way to do something and a wrong way. Don't take shortcuts. Don't tell yourself, "Well, I've got this knife in my hand anyway—why bother with a church key when I can just pry the lid off that jar with this?" What's wrong with that picture? Well, maybe you'll have time to figure it out on the way to the emergency room.

✺ Fire poses an ongoing safety concern in the kitchen. Grease fires are particularly scary. You should never fill a deep fat fryer to more than a third of its capacity. Also, any deep fryer you use should have a lid in case things veer out of control.

✺ This is so obvious it's almost insulting, but make sure you have fire extinguishers that work.

✺ Keep oven mitts handy at all times. One of the best oven mitts you'll ever find is a pair of welding gloves that you can get at the hardware store or an auto supply shop. They are made of thick, heat-resistant leather, and they come with long gauntlet cuffs that protect against burned wrists. Because they are designed to allow you to work with your hands while wearing them, they offer lots of control and flexibility. And they're cheap.

✺ When you take the lid off a pot, always lift up the far edge of the lid first. You could scald yourself if you do it the other way around.

✺ When adding food to hot oil, make sure that the ingredients are dry. Blot any moist ingredients, because the water will make the oil spatter, and you could be burned.

❦ Stand well to the side when you're opening an oven door. Five hundred degrees hitting you square in the face can really hurt.

❦ If you want to check an item that's in the oven, pull out the rack first. Don't reach in to get the item. The interior of ovens are very hot, remember?

❦ There is such overkill out there about using chemicals for cleaning, and so on. Too much exposure to chemicals can be really dangerous. It can result in allergic or immunological reactions. It's easy to get something like contact dermatitis, for instance, from chemicals. Think about experimenting with natural substances in place of some of those potentially damaging chemicals. Lemon peel or cinnamon sticks steeped in water can be a lot nicer and safer than those so-called "air fresheners." Maybe you can use baking soda to clean a surface instead of some caustic scouring powder. White vinegar works wonders on most things too.

❦ Never mix cleaning chemicals. You might set off a chemical reaction and produce something really dangerous, like chlorine gas buildup.

❦ One of the scary things that can happen in a kitchen is a gas leak. As soon as you smell gas, turn off the stove, open the windows, and have everyone go outside. Then call the gas company . . . from outside.

❦ If you're ever relighting a pilot light, here's something very important to remember: light the match first, then turn on the gas to light it. If you do it the other way around, the gas is accumulating, and that's a really bad idea.

Kitchen Fires

Fires are apt to break out in the kitchen—it comes with the territory. You need to know what to do in case that happens.

🌊 *On a range.* Immediately turn off the heat. Cover the pan, or douse with salt or baking soda. (Baking *soda,* not baking *powder,* which could make the fire worse.) Under no circumstances should you try to douse the fire with water or a Class A fire extinguisher. These will make the grease spatter, and you could be very badly burned.

🌊 *In an oven, a broiler, or a microwave.* Turn off the appliance, or disconnect it from its power source. Keep the door closed until the fire goes out.

If you cannot put the fire out easily, call the fire department immediately. Also, under no circumstances should you try to carry a pot or pan with burning contents to the sink. You could burn yourself or drop the pan, causing an even bigger fire.

This chapter is a beginning regarding the vital issues of safety and sanitation in the kitchen. Keep these issues foremost in your mind throughout your career. Stay informed, and stay on top of any changes in codes or new guidelines. Safety first . . . that's the motto.

Chapter 7

The Waiting Game

Why do people go out to restaurants? Think about it. Your first response might be "for the food." To a large extent, this is absolutely true. Customers certainly will not continue to go to a restaurant if the food is not good, but their tastes are not so elevated and challenging that they are looking for *Pâté de Foie Gras*, *Quenelles de Brochet*, or *Crepes Suzette*. Most of the time, diners will be perfectly happy with a good burger, some nice crisp fries, a well-done pizza, or some broiled fish. So if the food is not the thing that is primarily driving them to dine out, then what is?

The answer, when you think about it, is simple enough. People don't want to cook. And they don't want to set a table. And they don't want to clean up.

And they don't want to serve. They want to *be* served. They want to be taken care of. And they want that service to be as pleasant and responsive as possible without being intrusive. That's where the server comes into play.

If you are a waiter or waitress, a captain, or a bartender, this is the chapter that you will want to pay particular attention to, because it is filled with tips about how to do your job well. And the way to do your job well is, in a nutshell, to make your customers relaxed, happy, and satisfied. If you can accomplish this, then you will have the satisfaction of knowing that you have realized your potential in the work you have chosen to do, *and* you will be remunerated with generous gratuities in most instances. So let us begin.

"A" Is for Attitude

You've heard the expression "service with a smile," but have you ever stopped to consider just how important the thinking behind that expression is? It's not just a cliché, it's an absolute truth. A smile is the language that communicates your attitude, and if your attitude is not what it should be, then you need an attitude adjustment immediately. Let's hear what fellow restaurant professionals think about the issue of attitude.

❞ Some of the people I work with almost never crack a smile. And guess what? They don't get good tips. I smile like a jack-o'-lantern, and I bring the bacon home.

〰 I've heard people say, "But I don't feel like smiling." To that I say it's not a question of *feeling*, it's a question of *doing*. If you're an actor, and you have a show to put on, you don't say, "I don't feel like acting today." (Well, maybe you do, but then that's the end of your career.) As waitstaff, we also have a performance to put on. We are welcoming people in; we are creating a gracious and warm environment; we are making them feel wanted and comfortable. Nothing does that more quickly than a nice smile. You can polish a person's shoes for them, but it won't make them feel as good as a smile will.

〰 A good attitude will pay off in terms of smoothing over whatever mistakes you make. And, believe me, you *will* make mistakes. Everyone does. The water glass gets knocked over. You set a plate down in the wrong place. You're only human. But if you've conducted yourself like a human—warm and smiling and welcoming—then it's very unlikely that your patrons are going to hold anything against you. They're out to have a good time, not to give you a hard time.

〰 We're all a little sick of the young waiter/actor/whatever who comes over to the table and says, "Hi. I'm Michael, and I'll be serving you tonight." But you know what? It isn't so silly. In fact, in many instances it works. Giving yourself a name breaks down anonymity, and when you've broken down that anonymity, then you might get people to regard you as more of a human being, which in turn might translate into better gratuities.

🕮 You have to know when to stop. I'm a waiter, but sometimes, like everyone else, I'll go to a restaurant and I'll be waited upon. This summer, I was at a fish house on Cape Cod, and the waitress was one of those adorable, fresh-faced college kids. We started talking, and she was telling me how she goes to the University of Maine and was studying marine biology. Well, as cute as she was, by the end of the night I knew more about her than I do about my nieces and nephews. It was too much. A few details about your life, if it should happen to come out for some reason, might be very engaging, but that's it. People aren't there to hear your life story.

🕮 When it comes to human beings, there's no such thing as consistency. Everyone's different. If you have a traveler, for instance—someone alone, who's on the road—they might want to engage with you more than a family out to dinner will. If you have a very large group, such as at a banquet, they may barely even notice you and may even treat you as a non-person. It's not a pleasant experience, but don't take it personally.

🕮 You will, as a server, find yourself serving people that have had too much to drink and who don't know how to handle their liquor well. They may become rude or obnoxious. As their attitude changes, so will your own. You have to learn how to deal with these people, and in some cases that will mean appealing to your maître d' or manager for help.

🔊 The bottom line is this: the customer will not really care if you serve to the left or to the right. The customer will care if you seem like a nice, friendly, pleasant person. That's what the customer is looking for.

🔊 To some extent, attitude is determined by the kind of confidence you have, specifically about your knowledge of the food being offered. If you're serving a bouillabaisse that night, and your customer asks you what a bouillabaisse is, and you scratch your head and stroke your chin and say, "Beats me," you can be friendly and pleasant but you're still going to turn off the customer, because he's looking at you as some kind of authority about what's served in this restaurant. When you lose the customer's basic respect—which you will when you present yourself as a know-nothing—then all the smiles in the world [are] not going to bring it back.

🔊 Having some knowledge of the local area is helpful and will represent you as being a person worth reckoning with. Your customers might ask you about any local entertainment or sights of interest or road directions or whatever. Get informed—not to the extent that you're going to be a tour guide, but just enough to strengthen the connection to your customers if they should ask. They'll show their appreciation at the end.

🔊 You know that famous book *When Bad Things Happen to Good People*? Well, I'm going to borrow that for a second just to say that bad food happens to good eople too. Turning out food is not like turning out ball bearings. Things go wrong, and even with quality control in the kitchen, the patron may still wind up with a dish that just doesn't taste good. At that point, the management can correct the situation and can make up for the inconvenience by treating the patron to a free dessert or whatever. No harm done. But when a patron has bad service, it is entirely likely that he or she will never make a complaint to the management but will never return to the restaurant. There's a saying: "Good service can save a bad meal, but good food cannot make a customer forget bad service."

❝❞ Attitude is not just a personal issue, although clearly it is to a large extent. I mean, if you don't basically have a great personality and you're not really drawn to people, you're always going to have to work twice as hard to make it in a service profession. But attitude is also influenced by the overall feeling of the restaurant you work in. I've worked in places where all the servers are competing with each other as to who gets the biggest tips in an evening. It becomes a big game of one-upsmanship, with the customer almost an afterthought. I've also worked in places where everyone pools their tips, which are then equally distributed, and I really liked that. It created a harmony among us that boosted everyone's attitude, and we all wound up doing a better job, which meant that the pot got bigger and bigger.

❝❞ When we talk about attitude, we're not just talking about how you present yourself to the customers. We're also talking about how you present yourself to the management. The restaurant's goal is to do the maximum amount of business over the service period with as high a net profit as possible. If you sit around chewing the fat, then you're not going to help the restaurant achieve that goal.

🕮 Never engage in general conversation with other waitstaff when you're on the job. It's completely unprofessional, and there's no excuse for it.

🕮 Never join in on a patron's conversation. If they happen to be talking about Yorkshire terriers, and you have a Yorkshire terrier, don't get all excited and start talking about Yorkies. When a customer addresses conversation to you, then you can indulge, but only up to a point. Remember—you're there to serve, not to socialize.

Neatness Counts

An outward sign of your attitude is your appearance. It is obviously not pleasant to be served by someone who looks sloppy, unkempt, or unclean. Male servers should be clean shaven, with impeccably clean hands and trimmed nails. Female servers should wear their hair short or tied up. Both men and women should leave the perfume and aftershave at home and keep jewelry to a minimum. The uniform must always be spotless and pressed, and shoes should be polished. Choose sensible footwear—never sandals, open-backed shoes, or, unimaginable as this may be, high heels! And a word in support of support hose, folks—try it, you'll like it. They make a *huge* difference.

The Server As Seller

So you're a server. Guess what? You're also a salesperson. Now that description might freak you out. You—a salesperson? Salespeople are the ones who call you on the phone at night to sell you burglar alarm systems, or are those people in used car lots whom you can't trust. Get over it, and face up to it: the better you can sell, the bigger your tab will be. And the bigger your tab, the better your tip (not to mention the better the overall financial health of your employer will be).

What exactly does it mean for a server to be a seller, and how do you become good at it? Let's listen to your colleagues.

🔖 The selling thing is hard for some people . . . and hard for some customers. Some people come into a restaurant on a very fixed budget, and they resent it when you say "Would you like a cocktail?" or "Will you have dessert?" But most people don't resent it. In fact, most people expect it. They regard it as part of a server's job to suggest these things, and they're right. It *is* part of a server's job.

🔖 It's important to put your selling—or, if you don't like that word, your *promotion*—of the food into the context of the complete dining experience you're offering your customers. If you're the kind of person who can make Lobster Thermidor sound like tuna salad, then there's not a whole lot of point in your trying to sell something. Making something seem boring is the antithesis of promotion. But if you can rev yourself up to have a nice level of showmanship in your performance—an elegant, ritualized presentation of the wine; refilling water glasses; replacing soiled silver, and so on—then your customer will experience your selling as part of a generally expansive dining experience.

✺ Be informed about the food being served, and be passionate about it. If someone asks you what's good, don't say, "Everything." That's, like, so boring it goes in one ear and out the other. Compare the answer "everything" with an answer that goes something like this: "Well, you can't go wrong with anything on the menu, but the farm-raised pork chops with the chestnut-and-apple dressing is particularly special tonight. The meat comes from a small organic farm an hour into the mountains, and it's extremely fresh and flavorful." Now that's a description . . . and, chances are, that's a sale of a high-priced menu item.

✺ Telling the truth can be a very disarming way to make a sale. If your customer is ordering the turtle soup and you say, "It's a little salty tonight. I'd recommend the consommé," then that's a likely sale for you of what might be a higher-priced item. (And it's the truth—the turtle soup *was* too salty.)

✺ Always be a good listener. Don't rush the ordering process, no matter how busy things are. The customer has a right to ask questions, and if you get a customer who asks a lot of questions, that person might turn out to be particularly interested in food and might be particularly open to taking your suggestions.

🌀 When all else fails, suggest sharing. That might coax your customer to try something.

🌀 I've worked in some restaurants where they'll offer the customer a taste of something. Other restaurants will find that to be an atrocious practice. Make sure you check this with your manager before offering anybody any tastes of anything.

🌀 Once your customer has ordered, compliment him or her on the choice. They'll feel like they've done a good job and will want to do a good job again when dessert comes. In fact, compliment *all* of your customers as they order. They won't mind, and the complimenting can be subtle, not like you're giving them a pep talk. "Oh, *that's* one of my favorites," or "It's particularly good tonight"—that kind of thing.

Interfacing with Customers

No matter how good your attitude is and how expert you are at selling, issues will still arise now and then between you and your customer. You may hear complaints, and you will need to know what to do about them. Some suggestions from fellow professionals follow:

🌀 The customer is always right. The customer is always right. The customer is always right. Say it 100 times. Okay—in reality, we know that the customer is often wrong. When he asks for his grilled tuna steak well done, we understand immediately that he knows very little about tuna steak. When he orders a cola drink with Filet of Sole *Bonne Femme*, we understand that he knows very little about food, period. But we have to act as if he's right. That's the given in the relationship.

✆ When I got started in this work, a very experienced waiter told me that the key to being a good server is to be a fabulous fixer. There's a fly in the soup? Apologize—right away. Don't get defensive, and don't tell them it's a piece of grated carrot. Listen sympathetically to their trauma. Fix the problem as fast as you can (which generally means removing the offending dish and replacing it with something so wonderful that they'll forget the fly in the soup). Apologize again, and be extra solicitous throughout the rest of the customer's visit. Now that's a meal with all the fixin's!

✆ Don't take any customers for granted, even the ones who come in and order "the regular." Thank them often for their patronage. It means a lot to them.

✆ If something gets screwed up, either in the kitchen or on your end, don't bother explaining what went wrong. The customer doesn't care what went wrong. He's only interested in what goes right. Simply correct the problem and proceed.

✆ I've had customers who have become really good friends. I'm not kidding. They talk to me; I talk to them. But that's not a reasonable expectation. You're not looking to the customer to be your friend. You're there to *serve* the customer—don't forget it.

◖◗ If you have a very offensive customer, or a group that's very noisy or obnoxious, it's not your job to solve the problem. That's the manager's job. Go to the manager with your problem. That's what he or she is getting paid for.

These Phrases Might Work

If you find yourself in a sticky situation with a complaining customer, try some of the following phrases:

- Thank you so much for letting us know about this.

- I totally understand. I'd feel exactly the way you do.

- I'm so sorry. I'll take care of that immediately. And, best of all:

- I apologize.

Pet Peeves

We asked our restaurant professionals what they found most difficult to swallow when it came to customer interaction. Some of their responses follow:

- When they call me *garçon*. I mean, give me a break.

- The thing I hate most is when someone tells me to "smile." I smile plenty, but sometimes there are things going on in my life that make it hard for me to smile. I never act out about them, but I wish people would have a little more empathy.

- Some people think that if they're paying a restaurant tab, it entitles them to be rude. They leave off any kind of polite phrases, like "please" or "thank-you." It's not, "Where's the restroom, please?" but simply, "Where's the restroom?" Now that's nasty.

- What about these jokers who eat practically a whole dish and then return it to the kitchen because "something's wrong with it"?

- Don't you love it when a big group tells you they want separate checks after you've put everything on one tab?

- The worst? When a customer snaps his fingers. I want to dump the bean soup on his head!

Serving Young Children

Serving young children can be a challenge that calls for a few pointers. Your colleagues offer the following:

👐 Don't do for the kid what the parent is supposed to do. You're a server, not a babysitter. Don't place a child in a high chair or a booth seat. That's for his parents to do. If you happen to pinch his fingers or something, you're going to be the one who gets the grief. What do you need that for?

 Leave ice out of kids' water glasses.

 Don't include knives in a child's place setting.

And Now for the Work . . .

Having discussed things such as attitude and appearance, let's get down to the nitty-gritty of your work. Of course, we'll still have to speak in generalities. The range of restaurants—from Chez Snob to Maude's Diner—makes it impossible to address specific service issues. At Chez Snob, you will unfold your guest's serviette (napkin) and place it over her or his lap. At Maude's Diner, the customer helps himself or herself from the metal napkin dispenser on the table. But certainly many aspects of a server's job are consistent throughout this range. We focus on them now.

Setting the Scene

The server or busperson is involved in preparing the dining area. Let's hear from fellow professionals what's involved.

 Cleanliness first, of course. That means wiping the tables and chairs and making sure that the cutlery and the glassware are spotless.

One thing that particularly bothers me when I go to a restaurant are empty salt and pepper shakers. It's just that little touch that if it goes ignored I feel like, "Who's minding the store here?" Consequently, I am a fanatic about filling the shakers in the restaurant where I work.

I always keep a bowl of warm water at the ready, to which I've added odorless disinfectant—emphasis, you notice, on the odorless? That way, I can dip a cloth into it and deal quickly and discreetly with any messes that come up as I serve.

Keeping the water glasses and the pitchers filled with water is very important. It's about anticipation. A customer should never have to ask for water.

Check the floor, kids. The table can be nice and clean, but if you've got somebody coming in and there's a gum wrapper on the floor, he's going to remember the gum wrapper, not the clean table.

It's all about presentation. Not just the flowers (if you've got them), or the tablecloth, or the wineglasses, but also about whether the tables are nicely aligned and if the chairs are pushed close to the tables. That's all part of your job too.

Taking the Order

A *very* important part of the server's job is taking the order. Your colleagues comment:

A guest should never be seated more than three minutes without having a server approach. Three minutes is the absolute maximum. Set your timers!

❤ When you approach the table, offer a nice, friendly greeting. "Good evening. Welcome to the Cantina." Some establishments prefer something even friendlier, but I think most of us have gotten a little sick of the "Hi. I'm Dennis, and I'll be your waiter tonight" approach. I remember, years ago, when I used that "Hi, I'm Dennis" approach, and my customer said, "Hi, I'm John, and I'll be your guest tonight." Did I feel like a jerk!

❤ It's your job not only to point out the specials but also to make the specials *seem* special. Be prepared to describe them, particularly any that involve unusual ingredients or preparations. For instance, if you've got pasta in squid's-ink sauce—I'm not kidding, that's an Italian classic—you'll have to be ready to explain the special allure of this dish to wary patrons.

❤ If you're serving at a buffet, keep in mind that some of your guests may not be that familiar with the buffet drill. If they don't realize that the buffet is a separate option, make sure to bring it to their attention. Give them an enticing rundown of the dishes they will encounter on the buffet, with particular emphasis on the hot dishes and the desserts, as these are what will sell this higher-priced option. If they look undecided, offer to walk them through the buffet.

❤ Push drinks. If your guests are seated without having brought along cocktails from the lounge, suggest it to them. They won't be offended. "What can I get you from the bar this evening?" is standard operating lingo. Tell them that the bar is famous for their margaritas or strawberry daiquiris. And, of course, don't forget to check on who needs a refill.

📞 Always use a tray to carry a drink to a table. Even if it's only one drink. This isn't your living room. You don't carry a drink in your hand.

📞 Ladies first, when it comes to taking an order. That might seem old-fashioned and sexist to you, but it's still the way it's done. And, of the ladies, it's the senior lady who kicks the order off.

📞 It's very amateurish to forget who ordered what, so make sure you don't let that happen. Most experienced servers can rely on their memory, but if you don't yet feel that you can, try this system. Pick a spot to stand at by the table, and always take your orders from that same spot. Assign numbers to each seat in clockwise rotation, starting from your left. Indicate the seat number next to the item ordered on your pad.

📞 Many establishments today have computer terminals called "POS," or "point of sales" terminals, where the waitstaff enters all transactions into the computer, and the correct bill is printed for the guest. There's built-in control this way, because the waitstaff can't get any food or drink items without having entered the information into the computer. There's a remote printer at the bar or kitchen, and if the order isn't sent in, it's not going to print. Every item has to be entered into the computer, and this way the only way to steal is to partner up with another employee . . . not that I'm suggesting that!

🕮 If guests are taking their time making up their mind about what they want, suggest an appetizer. They're probably pretty hungry, and when you say, "Clams Casino," they may jump at the bait.

🕮 Suggest a wine order as soon as the meal order is placed. Know enough about the wines to offer some guidance, if requested. If no wine order is placed, remove the wineglasses.

🕮 Don't ever forget the selling. "The salmon is in season." "The duck has a special lingonberry sauce with it." And when your guest makes his choice, compliment him. "That's an excellent choice." It's so easy to say, and it'll make the customer feel good.

🕮 Always repeat the order back to the customer. This prevents confusion. Also, be sure to ask how your customer likes the dish prepared. Medium rare? Well done?

And Now Comes the Serving . . .

The proper serving of each course is part of the complete restaurant experience. If you know what you're doing, you can expect to be rewarded. Let's hear from fellow professionals.

🕮 Remember that you're a big part of the restaurant's quality control. Double-check each plate of food to make sure that the order has been correctly and completely filled. Better you should catch mistakes than the customer should.

🕮 Whenever you can, serve food from the guest's left. That's standard operating procedure. Food should be served with your left hand, as well, and should be cleared with the right hand. Don't reach over people, and don't ask people to hand you things. If they do, thank them.

🌀 Be quick about removing soiled or used items, including cocktail glasses, silverware, and so on. The debris of past courses should not be littering the table.

🌀 Some guests will inevitably use their dinner knife for the salad course. Don't take out your glove and slap them across the face. Simply remove the soiled knife and replace it with a clean one.

🌀 Never rush a diner! It's the prerogative of the diner to take as long as he or she wants to finish a course. If she's still having her soup when you bring out her main course, hightail it back to the kitchen with the main course to keep it warmed.

🌀 Make sure hot foods are hot. It's such a no-no to let foods become tepid.

🌀 Once you've served the main course, that's not the time for you to pull out a magazine and catch up on the latest gossip. You should continue to be monitoring the table closely. That means refilling water glasses, refilling wineglasses, removing empty cocktail glasses, and so on. If it's the custom in your restaurant, ask your diners how their meal is. Don't say, "Is everything okay?" It's a rather crude question and makes it sound like you're anticipating problems. It's better to say, "Are you enjoying your meal?" Most times you'll hear the affirmative. Sometimes you'll hear a complaint. Be prepared for anything and everything.

If your guest looks doubtful about the dish that's been ordered, try to find out why, in a low-key way. "Is this to your liking, sir?" "Is that the way you wanted it prepared?" Your job is to make sure that the diner doesn't go away with the problems unaddressed.

Remove bread plates after the main course. Doing this encourages the passage to dessert, which is exactly where you want your guests to go. Desserts are usually highly marked up, and your salesmanship really counts at that point in the meal.

You'll sell a lot more desserts if you can actually show your customers what the desserts look like. Hopefully your restaurant will have some kind of dessert trolley so you can do that. Encourage sharing if guests protest that they're stuffed. Make sure you highlight whatever is special about the desserts—your famous homemade ice cream or prize-winning tiramisu.

If your restaurant offers specialty coffees, don't forget them. They build up a tab nicely, and in cool weather particularly, they can be almost irresistible.

Is There Anything Else I Can Get for You?

The end of the meal is very important. It's that final impression that will factor in to your customer's overall experience and affect how generous a gratuity you will

Oops!

Spills come with the territory when you work in a restaurant. Even if you were a Gold Medalist in the Server Olympics, a spill will happen to you sooner or later (if not sooner). The issue is not so much avoiding spills—after all, accidents, by their very nature, are mostly unavoidable—but, rather, in how you deal with the spills once they've occurred.

📞 If some gravy or sauce is spilled on the table-cloth during a meal, first check that none has landed on any of the guests. If it has, offer the guest a damp cloth that he or she can use to rub out the worst of the mess. If the restaurant is at fault, consult with management. The restaurant may wish to pay for dry cleaning. If the spill is on the cloth, remove and replace anything in the area that's been soiled. Using either a damp cloth or a knife, mop up or scrape off as much of the spill as possible. An old menu can then be placed under the cloth, and one can be placed on top of the cloth, to then be covered by a clean napkin. Sincere apologies should be offered.

📞 If a guest knocks over a glass of water, first determine that neither the guest nor anyone else at the table is soaked. If the spill is significant, the party should quickly be reseated at another table, if possible, and allowed to continue with their meal. Otherwise, proceed with the steps mentioned above.

receive and whether the customer will be inclined to return to the restaurant. Some tips follow from fellow professionals for the final act:

◖◉ Check your guest check very carefully. Errors are embarrassing, and some customers may feel like you're trying to cheat them if the errors are in the restaurant's favor. If they have that feeling, you can kiss your tip good-bye.

◖◉ Make sure that every item served is on the guest check. Double check your addition, and include tax.

◖◉ Always serve the check on a tray, face down. You may sign the check with your name and with the words "thank-you" on the back. When you set the check down, say "thank-you" to your guest. Nobody ever minds a few extra thank-yous.

◖◉ It never hurts to introduce some new ideas to the management. I went to a restaurant where they presented the checks with little after-dinner mints. I thought it was a nice touch, and I suggested that we try it in our restaurant. People like it, and I think I've gotten bigger tips since we've started doing it.

The ABCs of Check Writing

Knowing the correct way to write out a guest check is of course very important. Keep the following in mind:

◖◉ Always use a pen, never a pencil.

◖◉ If there's a mistake on the check, drawn a line through it and have it initialed by your manager.

💿 Print all food items.

For food checks, follow these guidelines:

💿 Circle the number indicating the quantity in the left-hand column preceding the food item.

💿 Note the price in the far right-hand column.

💿 Compute and total food items (excluding the sales tax) before placing the check on the order wheel.

💿 Don't add on sales tax until everyone is finished ordering.

And a Few Words about Bartending . . .

We don't want to give bartenders short shrift. They are a very important part of the restaurant experience. But we're assuming that many bartenders will have had significant training in bartending courses, so our tips may not be as important to them as they are to other waitstaff. Still, let's look at some of the things all bartenders should be aware of. Your colleagues comment.

💿 Of course it takes a special kind of person to be a bartender. You have to like people. You're going to be a part shrink, part confessor, [and] part entertainer, *and* you have to know how to mix a Fuzzy Navel, *and* you have to be calm under pressure during Happy Hour when the crowds are flowing in. Not easy . . .

🍀 Bartending is not an art. Bartending is an exact science. That means that you never "free pour." You always measure out your drinks with a 7/8-ounce glass, and so on. If you free pour, you're likely to measure out too little, which can translate into customers going elsewhere, or too much, which can result in plummeting profits.

🍀 Okay, your guest comes in and asks for a "Carmen Miranda." You have never heard of a Carmen Miranda, and it's nowhere in your bartender's manual. What to do? Contact your manager to get clearance on the portion control and the price. (And hope nobody comes in that night asking for a "Russian Revolution"!)

🍀 Remember that you're more than "The Mixologist." You're also the one who's in charge of cleaning the glasses, the mirrors, the bottle stock, the bar top, and the shamrock. Those things had better be clean, because a beautiful bar helps sell drinks.

🍀 Never, never, *never* give drinks to employees at any time. Never sell drinks to employees at any time. Can we be any clearer on this?

🍀 This may be obvious, but I want to say it anyway. Don't make any substitutions without first asking your customer. If the lady orders a Pink Squirrel, don't tell her, "Sorry. No Pink Squirrels today, but I have a lovely Crimson Chipmunk for you."

🔊 Be friendly, be accessible, but be firm. A big—and difficult—part of a bartender's job is being able to say no when your customer has had enough. That takes practice, but you can't do the job without that piece of it.

Becoming a really good server is not something you can learn from a book. Experience is the real teacher, and part of gaining experience is making mistakes. Don't worry—everybody makes mistakes, and there are few mistakes, short of setting a customer on fire during a *flambé* presentation, that can't be dealt with. If you have the right spirit—if you really want to make people's dining and lounge experiences pleasurable— then you will succeed. This chapter is just a start—containing a few good and useful pointers that anyone working in the serving profession should know. Take the information, build on it, and practice your skills. The better you become at what you do, the happier your customers will be. And the happier your customers are, the more rewards you'll reap.

Chapter 8

More Members
of the Team

Most establishments of any significant size will have a layer of personnel that lies in between the waitstaff and the management—your maître d', host or hostess, reservations person, and cashier. All of these individuals perform tasks that are crucial to the successful operation of a restaurant, and they are often the first ones encountered by the public. It is therefore extremely important that they be trained to deal with people effectively, and that they know how to perform their jobs competently and confidently.

The Maître d'

The person known as the *maître d'*, short for *maître d'hôtel*, is at the top of the dining room pyramid. In fact, another name for this position is "dining room manager." The maître d' is responsible for overseeing the entire operation of the dining room.

As we discussed in the first chapter, back in the grand old days, the front of the house had a dining room brigade that allowed for the most exquisite and attentive service imaginable. Underneath the maître d' was a *chef de salle*, otherwise known as the "head waiter," whose job was to organize the service staff. Beneath the *chef de salle* was the *chef d'etage*, or the "captain," who took the guests' orders and saw to any special table-side preparations. Beneath the captain was the *chef de rang*, or "front waiter," and the *demi-chef de rang*, or "busperson."

Obviously, in all but the most exclusive restaurant environments, this hierarchy has given way to a considerably more streamlined approach. But although many restaurants today have lost the head waiter and captain positions, a great many have retained the maître d' or dining room manager.

Let's hear what's involved from the following professionals who hold that position:

❧ The maître d' is a very interesting and special job that has its two feet planted almost equally in the world of service and the world of management. In some ways, I see it as the single most important job in the restaurant.

🌀 Everything that applies to the waitstaff applies to the maître d'—only more so. If the waitperson has to be good with people, then the maître d' has to be that much better. If the waitperson has to be able to handle pressure, then the maître d' has to be cooler still. That's because the maître d' is modeling for the waitstaff. He or she is setting the example.

🌀 The maître d' does some of the same kinds of things as the waitstaff, but he does them with a flourish. He'll bend at the waist to check to see if a glass has a smudge on it, and if it does, he'll whisk the offending item away and have it replaced with a sparkling new glass. I once worked for a maître d' who went around fixing things that had absolutely no need of being fixed. He would summon over a waiter and in front of the guests would say, "This pepper mill is not as it should be. Bring me a better one!" Well, believe me, there was nothing wrong with that pepper mill, but he wanted to show the guests that he was looking out—in fact, *anticipating*—their every want and need. That's called "showmanship," and a good maître d' understands that the dining experience is meant to have certain dramatic quality. It should feel different than staying home with the ramen noodles. If it doesn't, then your restaurant is going to be in big trouble.

🌀 As the maître d', it's my responsibility to make sure that the service is first-rate. I'm completely involved with the training of staff. And the first thing I do is to make sure that my people understand what I consider the absolute no-no's. For instance, I've been a diner myself in establishments where they'll say they're open until 11, but when I've gotten there at a quarter to ten the staff will look at me like, "What are you doing here?" I once had a waitress actually start spray-cleaning the table next to me before she even took my order! I tell my staff that our last customer of the evening is to be treated every bit as graciously as the first and is entitled to enjoy his meal as leisurely as he desires to.

◖◗ I'm a maître d' in a top steakhouse in Chicago. I replaced a gentleman who was very into what I call "training by posters." He had posters up all over the place—"Top 10 Service Secrets," and so forth. You couldn't go to the bathroom without one of these things looking down at you. And did they do any good? Not a bit. That's why they hired me. Because I had a track record when it came to training staff. And how do I train my staff? By taking them through their paces over and over again, until they've got it right, and then refreshing the training as needed.

◖◗ The liaison work I do with the kitchen is an important part of my job. As anyone who works in the restaurant field can tell you, there's often a lot of tension between the front of the house and the back of the house. The front of the house thinks that the back of the house is egomaniacal and just dreams of going on the Food Network, while the back of the house thinks that the management is just hiring handsome boys and beautiful girls to wait tables and collect the tips. So I try to bring everybody together as best I can—to create a kind of family feeling. The best way to do this is to get people to eat together, and we plan parties for the staff too, or outings now and then, maybe to a vineyard or a farm or something. Recently, we all went on a visit to a purveyor who makes *foie gras*, and that was really interesting and helped build a feeling of solidarity.

☎ One of the things that a maître d' is expected to do is supervise reservations and the seating of guests. Nothing can possibly be more touchy than that. In the old days, you could get away with being very snooty and keeping the "commoners" waiting behind a velvet rope while you sat the "right" people. But these days the economy is so bad that nobody would be stupid enough to deliberately alienate any paying customers. So juggling reservations and seating is something that you'd better get good at in this line of work.

☎ As the maître d', I am very aware of setting an example for my staff. And that begins with my grooming and physical appearance. I tell you, when I see people coming in to work looking like they just got home from a Guns 'n Roses concert, I want to scream. I mean, puh-*leese!* I model grooming by going to a barber often enough to look styled and manicured and by making sure that my clothes are clean and neat *and* pressed. (Did this younger generation miss *ironing* or something?)

❧ Sometimes, as the dining room manager, I can't help but feel like "Big Mama." I've got the front of the house complaining to me about the back of the house, and vice versa. That's not good. My job is not to be Big Mama, but to be the coach and to try to get these people to act like we're on a team. Team members should never be blaming each other for things. Team members should be putting their heads together to figure things out.

❧ As the maître d', I take pride in the fact that I've been around the food world for a long time, and I pretty much know how things should be done. Like most people in this business, I've got a resumé as long as my arm, but the up side of that is that I've seen a lot of different ways of doing things, and I pick up good ideas wherever and whenever I can. I fully understand and am intent on communicating to my staff that the way to make it in the restaurant business is to offer a combination of quality and service. Sometimes customers remember the little things even more than the big things. Let me give you an example. When I got to my present job, I discovered that tea was served by putting a tea bag next to a cup of boiling water. Well, let me tell you, I put an end to that. It's the worst way in the world to make tea! You pour water *over* tea—you don't dunk a tea bag *into* water. Now we have a bunch of individual, single-serving teapots, and the customers love getting their own pot. Another thing is serving salad on cold plates. I absolutely hate it when I go to a restaurant and my salad comes out on this warm plate and I'm eating tepid lettuce. So in our restaurant, I've made it a rule that salad plates are always to be well chilled . . . as are the salad greens!

🕮 Attention to detail is so important if you want to be a good maître d'. I manage the dining room of a popular family-style restaurant in Milwaukee, and we get a lot of people taking home doggie bags. Well, a few of our customers complained that their plastic cartons opened up on the way and made a mess. What did I do? I gave them beautiful napoleons to take home, on the house, and I looked into getting better containers. I also instructed my staff never to pack hot foods and cold foods together. Always separately.

🕮 The maître d' usually handles food complaints. Here's my method. I'll go over to the table and the guest will tell me what the problem is. Usually he doesn't know what he's talking about—"the fish is off"—but I'll hear every complaint courteously and seriously. First order of business is to apologize, sincerely and profusely. Then I'll have the waitperson remove the offending item. I'll then offer the guest the menu and ask if he'd like another portion of what he ordered or something else altogether. A new check is written out, showing what was returned and what was brought in its place. More apologies are in order when the new dish arrives, and in our restaurant, we do not charge for alternative dishes (but that will depend on the policy in your restaurant). Also—and this is important—take every complaint seriously, and ask the chef to check the dish. If, in fact, there does seem to be something "off" about it—and surely this can happen—then you'll want to put an end to that dish before it goes any further and does any real harm.

📖 Tasting is part of the job. Frequent tasting throughout the day. Too much salt in the soup? Not enough salt? Sure, the chef is going to taste, but another set of taste buds never hurts either.

📖 The maître d' has to be the problem solver. That's the job. Let me give you an example. I've noticed, over the years, that one of the more awkward situations that can arise is when an order comes through wrong, and three out of four diners get their correct meals, but the fourth is left there looking stupid while his dish goes back to the kitchen. I've told my waitstaff that whenever this happens, they are to come directly to me, and I'll deal with it. And I do. I'll make a big fuss over the poor guy, and with the appropriate amount of ruffles and flourishes, I'll give him a nice appetizer or a soup on the house while he's waiting. Works like a charm every time . . .

📖 Dealing with lost or forgotten property is usually the province of the maître d'. If the property's been left behind by a regular customer, call her up. If you don't know the person who left it, keep it in the office. If it's a wallet, for instance, make out a list of the contents, and then sign this list and have it signed too by whoever found the wallet. Ask for proof of identity from anyone who comes to claim the lost property. After three months, if the property remains unclaimed, you can hand it over to whoever found it.

✍ What do you do if a guest suddenly becomes ill? That's another situation that will probably fall on the maître d'. So here's the drill: ask the guest if he needs help, and try to judge for yourself how serious the situation looks. Invite the guest into a quiet, private spot for a few moments, like the office, and keep his dinner warm. If the situation looks really serious, don't try to move the guest. Hand the controls over to whichever staff member is most qualified in first aid (you will have previously identified this member as part of your overall first aid and emergency plan). If necessary, screen the area off. Await medical attention, but allow other diners to continue with their meals, as best they can. It's very important that all accidents and incidents, no matter how minor they seem, be logged into an accident book. This is a way of protecting yourself against future claims against your restaurant.

✍ You're going to be dealing with problems right and left—get used to it. How about guests who drink too much? Well, if they come in looking like they're already three sheets to the wind, simply refuse to serve them. If someone is so drunk that they're coming in rowdy or inappropriate, summon enough staff to firmly, but not roughly, escort the person from the restaurant. In the case of the guest who has become drunk while dining in your establishment, you'll have to be firm here too and quietly and discreetly ask the guest to leave. If the person is obviously but *quietly* drunk, continue serving him his meal, but inform him that you will not be serving him any more alcohol. In all of these cases, write out a report, for the record. It's a good way to protect yourself.

🌀 Somebody's got to make sure that the rest rooms are clean, and if you take your work seriously, then that part of it is just as important as anything else. Do a periodic visit. An unclean rest room is such a turnoff!

The Hosts with the Most

Being a host or hostess in a restaurant is such an important job. You're not only involved in reservations and seating, but you're the first person the guest sees. Here is what our hosts and hostesses had to say about the job:

🌀 Appearance, appearance, appearance. Let's call a spade a spade: most establishments are looking for attractive people to work these jobs. If you've been hired, it's probably because you look and present yourself quite well. Don't start acting like the beautiful woman who once she gets her man starts lowering her standards and pads around in an old housedress. Every day you come to work should be like every night when an actor or actress goes on stage. You need to be impeccably groomed. Your clothing has to be spotless, and it has to fit you well and look very becoming.

🌀 Leave the perfume and aftershave at home. When a guest enters your restaurant, the first thing he or she should smell is the *Navarin of lamb* or the *Tarte Tatin*, not your gardenia cologne.

📞 Another way to describe who you are is "the greeter." Greetings are so important. A smile and a few kind words are absolutely essential. I hate it when I go to a restaurant and the host or hostess looks at me like I'm some unwanted relative who just showed up for dinner. Come on—get with the program! *It's so nice to see you tonight. Welcome to Waldo's. Brisk out there, isn't it? So nice to see you again.* (And you should be training yourself to remember faces and names!) These are the magic words, folks . . . or whatever versions of your own that you come up with.

📞 It's a hard job, because in a busy restaurant at a busy time, you've got a lot of hungry people waiting to be seated, but that's no excuse for you to start acting like a traffic cop. I've been to restaurants where the host or hostess will be barking things like, "Leave your name, and we'll call you," or "Sit at the bar until a table opens up." No graciousness, nothing pleasant. Personally, I find it inexcusable.

📞 It's important to be sensitive to the issues of solitary diners, particularly women. They'll often feel uptight about being by themselves. If you have room, offer them a choice—"Would you like a table or a booth?" The comparative privacy of the booth is usually appealing to them.

📞 You're going to be dealing with a lot of people waiting, and there are good and bad ways to deal with hungry, waiting people. A bad way is with a whip and a chair. A good way is to figure out some little amusement or surprise that will divert their attention. It helps, of course, if there's a reasonably sized waiting area, but assuming there is, get creative. At some point, I was handing out sketch pads and crayons, the way you would with kids, and people got a kick out of that. Circulating some nice wedges of foccacia can also work well.

📣 As [a] host, you may find yourself on the front line of dealing with certain unruly or rowdy individuals. Guess what group comes first to mind? You've got it—teenagers! I'm the hostess in a popular pancake house in Nashville, and I've gotten really good at spotting a troublemaker in a teenage crowd. I'll just refuse them service, and if they cause a problem, I'll call the police—end of story. I'll also call around to the nearby schools if I know who the kids are. Once this kid squirted ketchup on our walls, and the school made him come back and clean it up.

📣 Here's the bottom line on why hosts and hostesses may not often seem like the most pleasant people in the world: they don't make any money! Seriously, a lot of us only earn minimum wage, and when it comes to tips, I don't think so. I know that I, personally, came into my job thinking I was going to be more important than the waitstaff, and it was a rude awakening when I realized how much less I was making than they were. So I've asked my boss to put me in line for a server job. I'm no dope.

Reservations

Part of your work as a host or hostess may involve taking reservations. You also will be taking reservations if you are a designated reservations person. All establishments have their own ways of handling reservations, but a few basic standard operating procedures apply across the board.

📞 When the reservations phone rings, answer it by saying "Good morning" or "Good afternoon," state the name of your restaurant ("this is Chez Louis"), and ask how you can be of help.

📞 When you take a booking, make sure to get the following information: the day, the date, the name of the booking party, the number of guests in the party, the time they wish to be seated, any special requests (e.g., dietary restrictions, handicap issues), and a phone number where they can be reached. Then repeat all this information to the caller for confirmation.

📞 If a party calls up with a cancellation, repeat the information, to confirm it, and ask if the party would like to reschedule for another time.

📞 At the end of the conversation, say "Thank-you for thinking of Le Bistro. We look forward to seeing you." Or something of that nature that feels right to you and that will feel good to your future guest.

Cashiering

The host or hostess may be responsible for cashiering, or a separate cashier may deal with this aspect of the restaurant's operation. In either case, the same principles apply. Consider these tips on cashiering from your fellow restaurant professionals:

🌀 If you're going to be handling money in a restaurant, you should expect two things, right at the top. For one, you may be asked to sign a statement saying that any funds assigned to you are the property of the company, and that you, the cashier, will assume full responsibility for any overages or shortages. In fact, in a lot of states, there's no way that the employer is going to be able to enforce this, but the psychological advantage of putting the fear into the cashier is enough to motivate a lot of restaurants to use these signed statements. Also, many restaurants feel that anyone handling money should be bonded.

🌀 As a cashier, you should insist on having cashiering procedures written out and made available by the cashier station. Everybody needs to be on the same page—*in advance*—when it comes to handling money.

🌀 Before opening for the day, count the bank to make sure that the right amount of money is where it's supposed to be. Usually, the bank is maintained at the same amount, so if there are changes, you'll want to know why.

❦ Brilliant chefs can be slobs and use lots of bowls and throw things around, and nobody's going to care. Cashiers won't get away with such behavior. Neatness counts. That means when it comes to your drawer, all the fives go together in their special place, and all the tens, and so forth and so on.

❦ Remember that you're an important part of the restaurant, and that you may be the one responsible for the customer's last impression of your establishment. So be human. Always ask for a comment on the meal. "Did you like your lunch?" "Button up—it's cold out." Something nice.

❦ It's bad form to make guests wait at the register to pay their bill. If you can't help the guest immediately, for whatever reason, ask some other authorized person to help. If that's not possible, then at least acknowledge that you see the guest is waiting, and assure him that you will be with him in a moment.

❦ Here's how I do it: when a guest gives me a check and his money, I say out loud the amount of the check and the amount of the money I've been handed. I look at the bills carefully, especially any that are of large denominations. If a bill is a large one, I'll call our manager over. He's the only person authorized to make change for any bill above a twenty. He'll initial and date the bill. Of course, such policies vary from restaurant to restaurant.

❦ Always count out change twice—once as you take it out of the cash register and once as you hand it to the guest.

◖◗ Don't take any damaged, mutilated money, or any foreign coins.

◖◗ Of course, as a twenty-first century cashier, you're going to be dealing with credit cards . . . all the time. I know that whenever I find myself in a restaurant that doesn't take cards, I'm shocked . . . and, once or twice, have been in something of a jam. (Fortunately, I wasn't made to wash the dishes!) In fact, you may be seeing primarily plastic, so make sure you're on top of your restaurant's policies in that regard.

◖◗ At intervals—as you see fit—pull all the money not needed to make change, secure it with a rubber band or clip, and place the money and a slip showing the amount of the money in the safe, or ask an author-ized person to do this for you. These intervals should be varied so that no one can keep track of your habits.

◖◗ Make sure you never leave your station without locking the register. Also—very basic—keep your draw-er shut when you're not putting [in] money or taking it out. Those are the only two reasons for having an open cash register drawer. If some coins fall on the floor, give your guest new coins from the register, then close your drawer and look for the ones that dropped.

◖◗ Every establishment has its own policies with regard to cashing checks, but as a general rule of thumb, don't cash any checks unless your manager has written his authorization on them.

◖◗ Who takes register readings? Only authorized per-sonnel! That usually means the manager, assistant manager, or, if you are so designated, you. The same cast of characters are the only ones who can remove money from the register and place it in the safe.

✆ Always say thank-you, and look at the guest directly when the transaction is complete. This is not only polite to your upstanding guests, but it will make would-be thieves nervous, because they'll think you're memorizing their appearance.

✆ If you've had experience working around money with people, you'll see the worst that human behavior has to offer. There are a lot of crooks and short-change artists out there. One thing I've learned is to always finish one transaction before going on to another. These crooks will come in as a team, and one will try to confuse you while someone else slips their hands into the till. Don't let that happen!

✆ If you make a mistake or ring up something wrong during the transaction, just note it on your correction sheet, and then ring it up again—this time right.

✆ One thing auditors hate is when you make payments out of the cash drawer. The only times, in general, that you should be doing paid-outs is for tips to service staff that are charged against credit cards. These payments should be itemized on a waiter's tip sheet and signed for by the waiter when he receives his tips at the end of each serving period. At that point, the signed form becomes part of your closing documentation.

✆ When closing, count your total receipts, and set up your bank for the next day. The cash that's left over should be counted by denomination and noted on your deposit slip or envelope. You'll also be expected to prepare a daily report showing the amount of cash and charge sales, any tips paid out, and whatever else the management wants. Then you'll turn your deposit and your report over to the manager, or if you're in a large operation, maybe [to] a member of the accounting staff. For your own protection, keep a record book of the transaction.

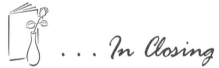

. . . In Closing

The staff we've focused on in this chapter and the last are the individuals who interface the most with the public. Before we leave this chapter, let's take a moment to review some very important concepts that relate to customer service.

📖 *Be detail oriented.* Some of the most memorable parts of a dining experience have to do with the little things. Flowers in the restrooms. Chocolates at the end of the meal. Signing the check with your name and the words "thank-you." Pay attention to details, and you will be rewarded for your efforts.

📖 *Fix, don't explain.* When people come to your restaurant for a pleasant evening and something goes wrong, they don't want to hear *your* side of the story. They couldn't care less. Explanations and defenses are not needed. Solutions are what the customer is looking for, and they'd better be good and fast.

🕮 *Be a good listener.* Nothing is more important than this. If you listen, you're more liable to get it right. If you get it wrong—if you bring out the chicken fricassee instead of the goulash or the apple pie instead of the peach cobbler—it brings the whole meal down.

🕮 *Speak the truth.* Nobody expects perfection. Be honest, yet discreet, and your honesty will mean a lot to your customer. If she's ordering the split pea soup, and you think it doesn't hold a candle to the minestrone, quietly direct her attention to that. "I just want to say that the minestrone is very special tonight. The split pea is nice, but the minestrone . . . *mmh.*"

🕮 *Make "thank-you" the two most important words in your vocabulary.* They work like magic. So does "I apologize." Those are real power words—never forget them.

Chapter 9

Bring on the Food!

In this chapter, we discuss the work of food and beverage directors and purchasers—those folks who bring food items into the establishment.

A large establishment generally will have a purchasing staff. The purchasers buy the food that will be prepared by the chef and kitchen staff. That food is then served by the dining room staff. The food and beverage directors review the procedures of the purchasers, the kitchen staff, and the dining room staff to make sure that all three systems are working together effectively so that the quality, economy, and presentation of the food are at its best.

Food and beverage directors also are responsible for scheduling the operating hours of restaurants and bars; sourcing suppliers of food and beverages; running cost comparisons; staying on top of inventory; analyzing trends; setting up purchasing and receiving procedures; checking the condition of what is received; keeping an eye on the competition; and hiring and dismissing workers.

These managerial positions are stressful and usually entail being on one's feet most of the day. The work can involve irregular hours, where one is supervising staff on different shifts. Food and beverage directors in large establishments, such as chain hotels, have to be very good at multitasking, as they often are dealing with conventions or large groups of tourists.

Let's hear how professionals who hold these kinds of jobs feel about their work.

❤❤ One thing I can say is that it's never boring. There's always some kind of problem that you've got to head off at the pass. Anybody who wants to be in this line of work needs to be a self-starter with a lot of initiative. You can't think of yourself as just a cog in the system. You *are* the system. The buck stops with you.

❤❤ The really important thing about this job is to be a team player, through and through. You've got a lot of problems coming at you every which way, and you need to be able to get along with people . . . or at least have people respect you. Most of us come out of the ranks, however, and this makes it easier. It's not like we're the second lieutenants who just got out of West Point and have never gotten our hands dirty, so people resent the heck out of us. We *are* those people, just moved up a notch or two.

✎ You're not just dealing with your own internal staff. You're dealing with suppliers and teamsters, and so you have to be able to relate to a lot of different kinds of people. Often in the restaurant business, it's such a model of the family—even when people are sniping at each other, they snipe the way you would in a family—but we've got a foot outside of the family, planted firmly in the outside world.

✎ Speaking a language other than English helps. Spanish, in particular. You'll be dealing with lots of non-English speakers, so make your life easier and pick up a little of somebody else's language, why don't you?

✎ I particularly like the trend-spotting aspect of the job. I have to say that I was pretty sharp when it came to anticipating the whole natural trend, with smoothies and soy milk and high-end juices and stuff. I made out like a bandit on those things.

✎ Like almost every other managerial or administrative position in the world, the biggest frustration has to do with personnel. There just aren't that many great people out there, and the turnover is ridiculous. Part of the problem is societal in nature. We just don't have the kind of social structure that they do in other countries, where there's child care and elder care and universal health care. I get a lot of people on my staff that are living on the margins of society, and when their kids get sick, they stay at home. I can't blame them, but what am I supposed to do? Have one person do the work of two for the same price?

Purchasing

The art of purchasing can be very tricky. How many lobsters to order? Four? Twelve? If you get stuck with too much lobster, *you're* going to have to eat it. And even though that lobster may be delicious, you're not going to get rich—or shine in your job—by eating your own inventory. Restaurant professionals offer some important tips on this subject.

💿 Okay, it's true that you can make a Chicken Potpie out of the chicken you didn't use for your Chicken Kiev, but not all ingredients can be converted so effectively and efficiently. Also, your chef may "quail," as it were, to the idea of Chicken Potpie on his menu, American harvest cooking aside. So the idea is to use the right quality product in the right amount at the right time in the right way at the right price. Got that?

💿 The key to this line of work is *forecasting*. I'm not talking about the weather here, although in a way it's not that dissimilar. Like the poor weatherman, the purchaser might think there's a hurricane coming—or an army of tourists on their way—and then something happens (a tornado maybe?), and nobody shows up. That's when you're stuck.

💿 The way that forecasting works is that you get your menu established and then you start figuring out the number of servings of each item that you think will be needed for each menu period. Obviously there's some value in being something of a math head here. So how do you approach the problem? Well, one way is to rely on history. What's the average number of dishes ordered in the past for that period? Then you might take into account other variables. Is it a holiday season? What's the economic climate? Are people opting for high-end dishes? Is it colder than usual this time of year, and are people looking for heartier fare? Then, of course, if your restaurant is new, you're struggling with the handicap of not *having* a history. Then you're relying on your overall experience in the business. In any event, forecasting is the name of the game. If you don't do it well, you'll order too much or too little. Either way, you'll lose. Like in any retail business, it's all about supply and demand.

📢 There's a whole lot to sort out before you start purchasing. You begin with standards—what quality of product is going to be used in your establishment? Are you the kind of operation that only uses fresh fish and fresh produce, or do you also use frozen fish and frozen produce, or even canned produce? Working with these standards in mind, you will then develop product specifications. These are detailed descriptions of what you are looking for and what you plan to use in your restaurant, and these are what the suppliers are held to.

📢 The point of product specifications is to get the kind of quality control you're looking for. Specifications should be detailed, in writing, and should cover issues like the amount to be purchased in the most commonly used units; the count and size of the items or units in its basic packaging; the common, trade, or brand name; the degree of maturity or stage of ripening; and things like that.

🕮 When ordering, you have to know your yield percentage. That's how much usable food you'll actually get out of what you buy. The formula for getting your yield percentage looks like this: percentage of yield = weight after cooking/weight before cooking × 100.

🕮 In drawing up your product specifications, you'll probably have to devote the most attention to meat (unless, that is, you've got a vegetarian restaurant). Seriously though, meat is, in most cases, the most costly item you'll be serving, so it's where you should plan on paying extra attention. You can get most of the information you need for your meat specifications from the Department of Agriculture, but the National Livestock and Meat Board also has some good stuff. You'll want to specify the cut of meat, the USDA grade, and the style (carcass, wholesale-cut, or ready-to-serve portion). Then you can start exploring issues like whether the beef is aged or grass-fed or kosher or whatever.

🕮 There's a lot to keep in mind when you're purchasing eggs. In most of the restaurants I've been involved with, we use frozen eggs for our baked goods. There's a nice price advantage there, and they work just fine. On the other hand, if you're operating a diner and you're serving sunny-side ups, you're going to want to use the freshest extra-large or jumbo eggs you can find, because that's going to make an impact on your customer, and the extra pennies you spend you'll get back many times over through word of mouth.

🔊 Some people judge a restaurant on the quality of the coffee that's served. Don't stint. A cup of coffee is usually the last thing tasted in a restaurant and will linger not only on the palate but in the memory. Coffee preferences are to a large degree determined by the kind of clientele you service. If you serve an elderly population, plan on fresh-brewed decaf, and lots of it. If you're in a hip, young area with people raised on Starbucks, coffee is going to count for a lot. Regionality is a factor too. In the Pacific Northwest, for instance, coffee is king, while in some areas of the South, you'll find people drinking colas at breakfast instead of java, so you'll know you won't have to invest in the most select coffee there. Choose a good coffee supplier, and get them to throw a good coffee-making machine into the deal. They'll often be willing to do that.

A Quick Guide to Buying Produce

The real art in purchasing is buying produce. So many mistakes can be made, and a grainy, mushy apple or limp lettuce leaves can bring a meal down in record time. Some helpful hints follow from the professionals:

🔊 Don't let your fruits and vegetables sit around. Some of them, like corn, begin to convert their sugars into starches as soon as they're picked.

◖◉ Take a crash course with your purveyor in what constitutes ripeness and how to best ripen fruits once you receive them. What should a ripe avocado feel like? A ripe persimmon? (You certainly don't ever want to go near an unripe persimmon!)

◖◉ Many fruits and vegetables bruise easily. The rule of thumb is to handle less, not more.

◖◉ Obviously you're going to want to look things over closely. Any soft spots, brown spots, insect borings . . . just move on to the next item.

◖◉ Familiarize yourself with how items are supposed to be packed. You don't want to be short-changed or discover that a layer of beautiful figs [is] acting as a smokescreen for the duds underneath.

◖◉ Acquaint yourself with sizes. Some fruits are sweeter when they're small, with the bigger items mostly used for display.

◖◉ Sometimes ugly is beautiful. I get old, bruised bananas for pennies, and then I peel them and freeze them and throw them into smoothies, where they work better than fresh bananas. Clever, eh?

◖◉ How much inventory should you have on hand? Ah, there's the age-old question. If we all knew the answer to that, we'd be rich. Generally, food items have a shelf life, which, if you're not 100 percent clear what that means, is the length of time the food can be stored without a loss of quality or weight. Fresh bread has a short shelf life; kosher salt has a long shelf life. Virtually any product that has water in it will shrink with storage, so there's no point in keeping a huge food inventory. Doing that will also tie up your dollars, and do you really want your dollars tied up in cans of beans that are going to sit on a shelf for who knows how long? So I'd say the general rule of thumb is that you should keep no more inventory on hand than what's needed to cover you from one delivery date to the next.

◖◗ When it comes to inventory, you've got to be careful not to overbuy. It's a human tendency. You think you're getting a great price on something so instead of getting 10 cans, you get 40. But then what if tastes change—your customers' or your chef's? You don't want to be stuck with 40 cans of lingonberry sauce that were just the thing for your Swedish pancakes six months ago, but six months from now, who feels like eating Swedish pancakes? So there you are, using up storage space, using up cash that could be put to better purposes, and you may not even be so thrilled with what you've got when the time comes to use it. Liquor is a good thing to buy in bulk if the price is right. That'll never go out of style.

◖◗ A food purchasing system calls for a par stock and a reorder point for each food item. For instance, the par stock for canned pears may be one case; the reorder point is when you get down to the specified amount. Something that's fast moving may have a par stock of 10 cases.

《◎ The purchasing is determined by the nature of the operation. If you've got a cafeteria in Sun City, Arizona, serving an elderly population, you may be using a lot of canned or frozen foods, and your reordering may be mostly on a monthly basis. If you have a *haute cuisine* restaurant, then you are dedicated to freshness, and you may be dealing on a daily basis with your produce suppliers and your butchers and fishmongers, not to mention the parade of specialty purveyors bringing you delicacies like chanterelles or rare cheeses or whatever.

Working with Suppliers

A big part of your job is working with the people who supply the foods and beverages you will be ordering—call them "vendors," "purveyors," "suppliers" or, if you are going right to the source, "growers" and "cultivators." Some good tips follow from professionals:

《◎ How do you determine who to use as a supplier? Well, the same principles apply as when you decide who to use to paint your house or fix your car. You're relying on reputation, word of mouth, referrals—that sort of thing. Who's got the most reliable service? Who's never going to leave you in the lurch? Who's got the best-quality product? Who's never going to try to cheat you? Who's got the best price? These are the questions you're going to be asking, and when you find some good answers, you'll know you have the right person.

✆ Always have backup suppliers in mind. There's not a lot of time in this business to start shopping around for new ones if your current supplier takes a powder or starts delivering bad goods. In fact, there's *no* time. So be prepared!

✆ A lot of places deal with full-line distributors, and certainly you can make a good argument for doing so. You get some nice specials from those folks, and when they introduce a new item, they'll give you training in how to prepare it. You save time in placing and receiving your order, because it's all computerized, and the billing procedures are usually very clear and easy. On the other hand, you may be bound to ordering certain minimum amounts, which can be hard when you're starting out, and you may wind up spending more if you're only dealing with one distributor. I mean, how are you going to do comparison shopping?

✆ I work for a large, natural foods restaurant in Burlington, Vermont, and I deal only with a food co-op. I love it! Everything is top quality, the prices are great, and the people are great. It's a not-for-profit organization, and there's a real political agenda behind it. People *care* about what they're selling, which is awfully refreshing if you ask me.

✆ One thing you've got to be really careful about when you're dealing with suppliers is quality control.

Ordering

There's an art to ordering as well. Let's hear how from restaurant professionals.

🕮 I always call around for competitive prices before I order anything. That's the way I was taught, and that's the way I do it.

🕮 My operation is small enough that I can do my own shopping, thank goodness. I have a cozy little café—really more of a tearoom—and I'm out and about getting what I need and really *looking* at things. Using my own eyes that way is half the fun of having a restaurant. Plus, you'd be surprised, but you don't save money dealing with a supplier. The supplier will factor the cost of delivery and the cost of providing credit and other services into your order, and so you're not going to get a deal at all. If I go, as a private consumer, to one of the giant discount warehouse operations, I can really save bundles of money and get a great range of choices in the bargain. I'll plan menus around what I find at those places—whatever's seasonal and affordable.

🕮 I order mostly from one supplier with whom I have a long and happy history. Maybe I spend a little more on certain things here and there, but so what? It's worth the peace of mind to know that I'm dealing with someone I can trust.

I mean, problems can come at you from the weirdest places. When I lived in Portland, Oregon, there were some restaurants there—not mine, thank heaven—that were dealing with a local sprouts grower. Everybody thought this guy and his farm were all peace and love and granola, right? But then there was an E. coli outbreak, and it was traced back to the sprouts. Now you're going to say, "Well, what about the health inspector?" But it can be months, or even years, before the inspector gets around to some guy who's selling sprouts or tofu or smoked trout or whatever. It all sounds lovely and homegrown and whatnot, but it can be deadly. You take something like peanuts. Some vendor brings you freshly roasted ground peanut butter. Great, you say. But raw peanuts can be infected with a fungus called "alfatoxin" that can permanently damage the liver. How'd you like to find yourself responsible for that kind of damage as a result of having dealt with the wrong supplier? If you're going to use these small suppliers, at least make an on-site visit to make sure they're not doing anything obviously terrible.

Receiving and Storing

The receiving and storing of foods is a very big issue for food and beverage directors and anyone else working in the area of purchasing.

Receiving

Creating a logical, coherent system of receiving is a very important part of your operation. Here are some valuable tips from those who work these jobs:

◖◖ The three basic methods of receiving are invoice, blind, and partially blind. With the invoice method, you'll get a delivery from your supplier that has—you guessed it—an invoice that specifies quantities, prices, and specifications for the order. Someone on your end will check the order against the invoice, and it's clearly a good hands-on method that's simple and fast. With the blind method, the order comes with a blank invoice or maybe an invoice that just lists the deliverables. So the job falls to you—or someone else in the purchasing area—to actually count the items and judge their quality. The supplier then sends a full invoice to the head of purchasing, and that person compares the full invoice to the one filled out by the person in his department who checked the order. Any discrepancies are then reported to the supplier. With the partially blind method, the delivery comes with an invoice that is as complete as with the invoice method, except that the quantities are not specified. The purchasing clerk counts the items and notes them. So there you have them, and it all depends on the operation you're in.

◖◖ When receiving, inspect your items thoroughly, count quantities, check for any damaged containers, and keep an eye out for any items that might have to be repacked. You can't just use your eyes. You've got to use your nose, and you have to use your hands to go through these boxes.

🔊 I always take random sample temperatures of any refrigerated or frozen foods I receive. You've got to be so careful about that. Your refrigerated foods are meant to be delivered below 40°F, and your frozen foods should come in at 0°F or below. If your thermometer tells you differently, don't accept! (And another thing: have a bunch of thermometers at the ready, and make sure to resanitize them between checks.)

🔊 Bad frozen food announces itself quite clearly. You'll see large, rocky crystals of ice where there shouldn't be any, or whole solid areas of ice, like little glaciers, or discolorations on the food, or packages that have been bent out of shape by the thawing and refreezing. Just say no to these.

🔊 Have a look at your supplier's trucks. What's going on in there? Are the raw meats separated from the produce and the ready-to-eat food? Are the refrigerated sections good and cold?

🔊 Pay close attention to expiration dates and government inspection stamps. That's what they're there for.

🔊 Be very attentive when receiving dry goods for any signs of moisture or insect infestation. Cereals, grains, dried fruits, sugar, flour, rice—all that stuff should come in dry, unbroken packaging.

🔊 Sure, you've heard this a million times, but for the record, let's say it again. No cans with swollen sides or ends, no missing labels, no rust, dents, or anything of the kind. These could be signs of botulism. And that's life-and-death we're talking about folks.

🔊 When it comes to meats, you're going to have to tag all wholesale cuts. The tags come in two parts. One part stays on the meat; the other part goes to accounting. The tag should identify the supplier, the cut, the weight, and the unit price. You'll use it to ensure your FIFO system of inventory control—First In, First Out. A very central concept when it comes to perishables.

🔊 Date all your items. That will allow for FIFO inventory control. And when you shelve the items, put the new supplies behind the older ones, so that the older ones get used first.

🔊 Send all your items immediately to the storage area. Nothing should be left sitting around where it doesn't belong.

Storing

What can we tell you about storing? A lot! The professionals speak:

🔊 Your first line of defense is to keep your foods out of the danger zone. What's the danger zone? Between 41°F and 140°F. That's where contamination starts to happen.

🔊 Food *only* goes in its proper storage area. It doesn't go on the shelves about the stove or on that extra shelf in the bathroom, even if it's in cans. Understand?

🔊 Your options are to store foods in their original containers or to repack them in tight-fitting, leak-proof, pest-proof, nonabsorbent sanitary containers of your own. But of course once you start repacking, the chance of contamination increases.

📞 Don't forget to label and date your products. And rotate them on the shelves so that the old—or should we say "older"?—gets used before the new.

📞 Keep your storage areas clean and well lit. You've got to be able to read your labels!

📞 Do frequent tests of the temperatures in your temperature-controlled areas. And, also, remind everyone who works in the restaurant that traffic has to be kept to a minimum in the cold-storage areas. If it's going to be like Grand Central Station, with people going in and out all the time, you're never going to be able to maintain the necessary temperature.

📞 Clean up any spills or leaks immediately, and remove the dirty packaging and trash from the premises as fast as you can.

📞 Store all cleaning supplies and chemicals away from your foods, and make sure they're in the original packaging or that they're repackaged in clearly labeled containers.

📞 Ideally, storage areas should be close enough to the kitchen so that they can be checked several times a day. You want to be able to easily see what's going on in those areas.

📞 Does your storage area need a makeover? Stained and rusty metal shelves can support bacteria you know. Holes in the walls or floor allow mice and rats to come and go freely.

Unacceptable Foods

Okay, you've gotten a bad batch of something. Now what do you do?

📢 Keep the bad stuff at a distance from the good stuff.

📢 Turn to your purchase agreement and product specifications to back up your complaint.

📢 Never throw away bad items or allow the delivery person to remove them until a signed adjustment or credit slip is transacted.

📢 Make a notation of the incident in your receiving log. Note the item involved, the specification that was not met, and what type of adjustment was made.

📢 If this sort of thing happens too often, get a new supplier!

📢 Train your staff! Make sure that everyone's on the same page with regard to these storage issues. That's the big thing.

Well, there's a start on the important issues that face anyone involved in food purchasing. We now move on to managing, a very challenging job indeed.

Chapter 10

Managing Your End

As a restaurant professional, you may currently be in a managerial position or perhaps you've been asked to take one on. If you're not quite there yet, then maybe you've set that as a goal for the future. In any case, if you're the kind of person who likes a challenge, then being a manager is right up your alley.

In this chapter, we explore the various aspects of a manager's job. The information here pertains just as well to assistant managers and banquet managers as to general managers. All of these positions require similar talents and strengths, so let us state at the outset that we speak in fairly general terms. We start with two fundamental questions: What does a manager do? What makes a *good* manager?

The Job

Whether you're a restaurant manager, an assistant manager, or a banquet manager, the tasks are generally quite similar. Let's hear from the managers themselves about what's involved.

🕮 I'd say the #1 priority of this job is controlling costs. Hey—they don't call it "the bottom line" for nothing.

🕮 Cost control and financial management is definitely way up there at the top of the list. There's so much theft and pilfering and waste involved in this business, it's unbelievable. You know the old joke—how do you make a small fortune in the restaurant business? Start with a large one. Seriously, if someone's not keeping a close eye on things—and that someone should be the manager—then the ship is going to sink.

🕮 If you ask me, the biggest part of the job is the operations management. You're there to make sure that the shifts are run smoothly and efficiently.

🕮 I like to think of myself as "The General" (hey— I'm entitled). I manage banquet operations at a huge hotel in Dallas, and I pull together all the communications between my assistant managers, my supervisors, purchasers, and all the other team members in my organization.

🕮 Let's not forget that keeping up good customer relations is an important part of the manager's job.

You're the one who should always be looking around, seeing to it that everybody's happy.

🎕 For me, it's so much about personnel. Hiring, firing, motivating . . . getting people to do their best and dealing with people who are doing their worst.

🎕 My favorite part of the job is the training. I'm really good at it. I can communicate what's involved in peak performance, and I can turn someone very green into a ripened professional in fairly short order.

🎕 A restaurant can be a pretty insular world. As a manager, I look outside that world. I interface with our corporate superiors. I interact with others in the broader community, like the media and various government agencies. I try to see the big picture as best I can.

🎕 A very important part of the job is assuming primary responsibility for making sure that the facilities and equipment are kept in top shape. Matters of safety and hygiene become matters of life and death in a restaurant setting. I take that as seriously as it demands to be taken.

The Makings of a Good Manager

What does it take to succeed as a manager? What personal characteristics should one possess? Let's listen to the professionals:

🎕 I'd put problem solving at the top of the list. To be a good manager, you have to be a good problem solver, because that's what you're doing all day long, day in and day out: solving problems.

🕮 You want to be flexible. Rigidity is counterproductive. Be open to hearing new ways of doing things. Good ideas can come from all different directions, many times from the direction you'd least expect.

🕮 Having a real sense of responsibility is so important in a manager. I'm not talking just about responsibility for your own performance. I'm talking about taking responsibility for *people*, and knowing how to build a sense of responsibility and initiative in them.

🕮 You have to know how to motivate people. Generally, that happens by setting a good example.

🕮 A healthy competitive streak never hurt in a manager. After all, the restaurant business is highly competitive by nature. You have to always set out to do your personal best and to do one better than the next guy.

🕮 You have to have something of a thick skin. You're going to suffer disappointments and failures in this business. You can't let them get the best of you. Today may be a bad day. Tomorrow could be the best day of your life.

🕮 You want to be prepared. You want to look ahead. You want to anticipate. Preventing problems is easier than fixing them.

Controlling Costs

We identified cost control as one of the key issues in a manager's professional life. Whole books—*many* whole books—have been written on this topic, so we won't get into the nitty-gritty of things such as Food-Use Analysis or procedures for Daily Sales Analysis. We do want to talk in broad strokes, however, about some very important aspects of cost control.

Controlling Labor Costs

Too often, a restaurant's profits go down the sinkhole of personnel problems. Later in the chapter, we hear hints on training, which can alleviate a lot of problems if done well, but now let's hear some tips from professionals on good ways to make the most of staff.

✆ Start with a job manual, and make sure that there are definitions and responsibilities listed for every job. Hold your employee to the manual.

✆ Hire the right person for the job. Un-hiring is so much harder to do than hiring well to start out with.

✆ Give careful thought to what you realistically need in terms of staff. Don't overstaff. You're not Versailles, you know.

✆ Train, train, train. There's no substitute for good training . . . and continued mentoring.

✹ Consider your scheduling methods. You may be scheduling too few or too many employees on any given shift.

✹ Examine your systems to determine how efficient and effective they are. Match people with equipment. Invest in time-saving equipment if you can, but if you do, make sure you train people well in their use.

✹ Keep your knives and blades sharp. That will reduce accidents sharply, will save time in the kitchen, and will lower your insurance rates.

Controlling Food Costs

Need we tell you how much money you can waste on food? Yipes! Some strategies follow from managers to keep you in line on that front:

✹ Start by reviewing your menu very carefully. It may be swell and glitzy and exciting for the customer, but are you wasting food?

✹ Controlling food costs has so much to do with purchasing methods. Are you getting competing bids to assure the most advantageous price? Are you specific enough when placing your order? Are you losing food items through spoilage or other indications of improper storage?

✹ Do an analysis of your food preparation methods to see if you're incurring unnecessary costs that way. Which brands and quantities are giving you your best results? Do yield tests to determine what your true costs are. And do all of this on an ongoing basis.

🔊 Follow your recipes. Food costs escalate when cooks and bartenders make up their own recipes or measure out ingredients "by eye" instead of by measuring spoon.

🔊 Run regular audits to determine what's what. Audits are going to be the thing that lets you know if there's been a hand in the till.

🔊 As a manager, I do daily inventories of our expensive stock.

Pilfering

There's petty theft from the cash register, and then there's petty theft from the larder. It's a big problem in restaurants. Here's how to protect against it.

🔊 Keep all doors locked, except for the guest areas.

🔊 Make sure that food storage areas are kept locked.

🔊 Be clear on who has the authorization to be where.

🔊 Check the trash to see what's been thrown away. If you find empty cartons of items where they shouldn't be, you can assume that something's not right.

🔊 Have employees stash their personal belongings in specified places, such as lockers.

Controlling Overhead Costs

Overhead expenses are another sinkhole you have to watch out for. Consider the following advice from professionals:

📞 You wouldn't believe what people will "help themselves" to. Toilet paper? Paper towels? Just watch how fast that stuff goes. Keep it all under lock and key, especially office supplies. That's a real favorite for pilfering.

📞 Watch out for telephone use. Develop a policy, and stay with it.

📞 Let your staff know what things cost. I post our monthly invoices. Electricity, water, heat, insurance, rent—let them see it all, and let them know that if we can economize on these expenses, then they may reap some benefit from it.

📞 Repairs and maintenance can become a big area of expense. Check with your staff to see if anyone is unusually handy. You can compensate that person for his or her time, and it'll probably cost you a fraction of what it would cost to bring in an outside contractor.

📞 Serviceware breakage can also become a serious cost-control issue. Maintain a Serviceware Replacement Chart on the wall near the dishwashing area. Direct your staff to enter any broken items as they occur.

📞 Try to alleviate the breakage issue by starting out with staff that handles things carefully. Some people, tough as this may sound, are just plain clumsy. Handling dishes is not a good job for them. You'll also want to determine if your serviceware is up to the job. Some crockery and china is just not very well made or sturdy.

◖◗ Check into magnetic trash can traps. These will catch most silverware before it's accidentally tossed.

◖◗ Pounce on any waitstaff you see carrying the notorious "glass bouquet"—four or five water [glasses] or wineglasses in their hands. Dishwashers and bartenders should be carefully trained in how to carry and clean glassware the right way.

◖◗ Check the garbage frequently to make sure that broken items are not discarded without having been recorded on the replacement chart. Some people try to cover their tracks, and that just won't do.

◖◗ I keep a memorial pile of broken dishes in our kitchen, so that people see how much waste is involved.

◖◗ We play a training game every now and then. It's a variation on *The Price Is Right*. I put out everything that the staff uses and abuses—napkins, plates, glasses, sugar packets, crackers, and so on. I put these in front of the team with a card, facing down, that has the price of each item written on it. Then I make up teams of two, and whichever team gets the most right answers gets a perk—a bottle of wine or something. It's fun, and it really makes the point.

Personnel

Certainly one of the major functions of a manager's job is to deal with personnel. That means hiring them, motivating them, and dealing with problems that arise.

Hiring

So much pain and trouble can be avoided by hiring the right person for the job. Easier said than done, you reply. Well, it may not be easy, but it *is* possible. Some thoughts from managers on the subject follow:

📖 Before anything else, you need a philosophy about hiring. Mine goes like this: I look for people whose image and attitude fit my restaurant, who present themselves as "people" persons that know how to get along on a team, and whose lives are not so complicated that they're going to make my life more complicated than it already is. End of story.

📖 I find that the best way to get new staff is through referrals from current employees. Great people tend to know great people—at least that's been my experience.

📖 Get referrals from your staff by offering them cash or other incentives. If you bring in someone good, you get 100 bucks or 500 bucks or two tickets to a game or a gift certificate to a department store or whatever works for your establishment. Give the rewards immediately. Instant gratification works! And make sure your staff knows about these incentives. Don't keep it a secret.

≈ Don't forget about former employees who were good. Keep a file on them, and check in with them periodically. Sometimes an overture like that will work to get them back. It's worth the trouble in a lot of cases.

≈ Face up to it: in this business, you're going to have personnel issues. There's no two ways about it. That means you may have to be adventurous. In our city, we had a big influx of Croatian immigrants, and I made a point of penetrating that community. I hired one, then another, then someone's cousin. Sure, we had some language issues, but they were really good workers and weren't as spoiled as a lot of the workers I deal with.

≈ Make alliances with your local high schools and colleges. Culinary colleges, in particular, are ideal places to find high-quality employees. These students tend to look closely at quality-of-life issues, however. Expect to have to give bonuses to defray relocation costs and tuition bills.

≈ Set up a hotline so that applications can be taken on a 24/7 deal. A person should be able to call at any hour to say, "Is there a job for me?" Because, as you well know, there usually is!

≈ When it comes to advertising, I stay away from newspapers. Frankly, I'd rather post a notice on the bulletin board in a laundromat. The Internet's pretty good though. I've gotten some nice people that way.

Interviewing

Interviewing is an art, both for the person being interviewed and for the interviewer. As the interviewer, brush up on your skills with the following tips for managers:

⟪ When you're hiring for a job, be clear about the job. What's the best way to be clear about it? Have a job profile or job description available to you. If you're working in a corporate structure and the job descriptions come down to you from the Human Resources Department, review these descriptions regularly to make sure that they're still up-to-date and accurate.

⟪ When I interview, I take the reins and start out by giving a thorough description of the job I'm looking to fill. I want the person to know right at the top exactly what's expected. What are the day-to-day responsibilities? Who is that person going to be reporting to? What are the opportunities for advancement? No point in wasting time if the candidate doesn't like the sound of the job.

⟪ An interviewer is like a journalist. You have to ask good questions. That means that you should avoid questions that can be answered with a "yes" or a "no." Don't say "Do you like being a line cook?" Ask "Why do you *like* being a line cook?"

⟪ I always ask a candidate to describe a situation in which he or she had a conflict with someone and to tell me how it was resolved. Boy, you can learn a lot from the answers you get to that one.

⟪ There are a lot of questions you can't ask—a person's age, religion, sexual preference, whether she's

ed, or divorced, whether the worker
d for workers' compensation, whether
ver had cancer or been in a drug-treat-
—but that's okay, because there are a lot of
good ons you *can* ask.

Good Questions to Ask a Job Candidate

We asked around, and our managers revealed their favorite questions, including:

- Tell me something about yourself.

- What are your duties in your present job?

- Describe your "dream" job.

- What's your favorite restaurant, and why?

- Are there any times in particular that you cannot work?

- How do you feel about working overtime?

- How do you plan to get to and from work?

- Where do you see yourself three years from now?

- Do you have any hobbies? Play any sports?

- Do you speak more than one language?

- How would you handle a drunken customer?

- What do you think are your greatest strengths and weaknesses?

- Tell me why I should hire you.

- What do you know about our restaurant? Why do you want to work here?

- Give me an example of an unusual request from a diner. How did you handle it?

This is a start. Clearly, you'll have questions of your own!

Motivation

Now that the hiring is done, how do you motivate your new employee (or recharge your employee of long standing?). This is a very important subject for a manager. Let's see what our professionals have to say.

◖◖ Motivation leads to retention, and in this business, where personnel sometimes feels like a revolving door, retention is key. I don't know any better motivator than money. If you do, I'd like to hear about it. That means you've got to compensate competitively. Check cost-of-living indexes in your area, and adjust as needed on a regular basis. Of course, compensation involves all kinds of other benefits as well, so think creatively too.

◖◖ People really want to enjoy their jobs. That's not so much to ask, is it? So make the environment fun, as best you can. Of course, the idea of "fun" will vary from one restaurant to another, based on a restaurant's style and personality. Maybe waiters on roller skates makes sense for you. Maybe you can drop the uniform and let your waitstaff dress as they want. Who knows? Experiment!

📞 Let people know they're appreciated. Tell them! Start a little newsletter with interesting tidbits about people's accomplishments on and off the job. You can do it on your computer. It's easy and so effective.

📞 Nobody likes a boring job. If, as a manager, you recognize that a job *is* boring, come up with some ways—other duties, specifically—to make it less so.

📞 Work the floor. Don't sit in your office waiting for someone to come to see you. Be out there. Encourage input and feedback. Ask for suggestions. If you ask, you'll get them.

📞 Call people by their names. Forget the "hons" and "dears." It's sexist and stale, and it doesn't make people feel warm. It makes them feel small.

📞 Write nice notes to people. It's really nice when you slip a note like that into a person's paycheck envelope. *Great job the other night, Lee. You're growing by leaps and bounds, Fritz.*

📞 Model, model, model. Don't just rely on a mission statement posted on the wall to show that you care about quality. Show by your actions that you care about quality.

📞 If you can move toward flexibility in your scheduling, then do it. In the world we live in, with dual-career couples, that means so much.

📣 Give rewards, treats, and prizes for achievements. People love it! Throwing a staff party every now and then, with awards like "Rookie of the Year," builds team spirit and motivation enormously.

📣 Whenever the restaurant has a seriously "off" night—and we all do—and your staff is feeling completely frazzled the next day, sit around and talk about it. Figure out what went wrong. Soothe people's feelings. That's the job.

📣 Discuss sales, cost control, and goals with your staff. They like to feel that they're important enough for you to share this with them . . . and guess what? They *are* important enough!

📣 Everyone makes mistakes—*everyone*. Including you. Be tolerant of people's mistakes, and help them learn from them.

📣 Reinforce a good job with praise. *I liked the way you dealt with that customer. You really kept a cool head last night. You did a beautiful job cleaning up that mixer.* By the same token, be very specific about what you don't like. Don't personalize it and say, *You clumsy fool.* Instead, try saying, *It's not a good idea to carry glasses that way.* If the bad behavior continues, and glasses keep breaking, you're well within your rights to show some irritation and say something like, *This can't go on this way. Are you interested in working here or not?*

📣 Your personal problems belong at home. Had a fight with the wife? Don't pick one with the cook. Got that?

♨ The community of the restaurant is modeled on the family. It's very intimate, because any situation where everyone eats together is going to feel like a family, to some extent anyway. Don't make it worse by having your "favorites." It's going to bring up a lot of sibling stuff for certain people, and you're going to have problems as a result.

♨ Be a *mensch* about how you terminate an employee. If you act like a thug, rushing someone off the premises, it can easily spook the rest of your staff.

♨ Always conduct exit interviews. Find out why a person has decided to leave. Where are they going? What are they looking for that they couldn't find here? Don't get defensive or angry. Just listen—you'll learn something.

Bad Apples

In every bushel, you'll find a few bad apples. In every restaurant, your staff will include, at some point or another, some bad apples too. What do you do about it? The professionals offer their advice.

♨ You know the type—they've always got some problem going. Real malcontents. If it's not something at home, it's someone they work with. If it's not someone they work with, it's the temperature or the smell or the restrooms or the customers. They make me crazy!

ᐷ You've got to bite the bullet and confront them. Have your facts ready. Keep a list of your "grievances" against the person, and present them at the right time. Control yourself, and don't do it in a state of high emotion. Be calm and factual.

ᐷ The confronted "apple" will often try to turn the tables and tell you everything that's wrong with you . . . or someone else on the team. Don't buy into it. Bring them back to the point of the talk—which is that it's about them.

ᐷ If you can get the "apple" to own up to the behavior, and if you don't want to outright fire them (some bad apples actually perform their jobs well), you can get empathetic. How can I help you with this? Do you need more training? What's causing the problem? If they don't own up to it, set a timetable for improved attitude . . . or else. Document this in a follow-up note.

ᐷ Don't procrastinate. Bad apples don't go away. They just continue to rot until the whole basket is spoiled.

Training

Training is vital to your operation, and we wouldn't dream of offering you a crash course here. You'll have to devote much more time to reading and continuing education to discover the training methods that will work in your establishment. But we don't want to leave this chapter without offering some tips from managers about staff training.

☜ Know the job in and out before you try to train anyone for it. You'd be surprised at the gaps in your own knowledge.

☜ Let your staff know exactly how they can expect to benefit from this training. Clue them in to the objectives.

☜ Determine what your staff already knows going into the training. There's no point in wasting everyone's time teaching them something that's already been mastered.

☜ Establish a time frame for the training. Is it an hour? Is it a day? Don't let it be open-ended.

☜ Recognize that the training may not pay off with immediate results. Sometimes it takes a while for learning to kick in.

☜ Different people learn at different rates. That's only human. And when things like language difficulties enter into the picture, the rates really differ.

☜ When someone makes a mistake, first compliment them on what they did right before you correct them on what they did wrong.

☜ Training doesn't have to be so formal or so set in a particular time and place. It can—and should—be going on all the time. In a quick conversation, in an e-mail. And it should always be light and fun—or at least as much of the time as you can make it feel that way.

As a manager, you can't be everywhere all at once. Make sure that you're continually training your assistant managers to take on increased responsibilities.

You want to hear a really terrible idea? All-day training sessions or any kind of marathon encounter in which a person is supposed to learn for hours at a stretch. Let the learning come in short chunks. Think about learning golf, for instance. Do you want to take a five-hour class in driving a ball, or would you rather have 10 30-minute sessions spread out over a month? Duh . . .

Running a Meeting

As a manager, one function of your job is to preside over meetings. A weekly meeting would probably include discussions of team performance, comp sales, service, safety, repair and maintenance, and more. There is a right way and many wrong ways to go about these meetings. Some tips from managers for getting it right follow:

Think "agenda." Never schedule a meeting without an agenda, and stick to it religiously.

Set a start time and an end time. And make them very real.

Make sure you don't go into the meeting unprepared. Don't forget—you're always modeling, or at least should be!

Schedule the easy-to-take-care-of stuff at the beginning of the meeting. Swift action on easy topics gives people a sense of accomplishment that serves them well as they go on to tackle harder issues.

✆ Have a set policy, understood by all, on how decisions are actually reached.

✆ Make sure someone is taking notes or minutes. All of your meetings should be "for the record."

✆ Make interruptions a no-no. If you feel it would work well, have people raise their hands to talk.

✆ Personal attacks have no place in these kinds of weekly meetings. Put a swift and decisive end to such behavior.

✆ Let people know that sideline discussions are highly distracting and counterproductive.

✆ Remind everyone to turn off their pagers and cell phones.

There is so much more to say on the subject of managing. It's a big job, truly multidimensional, and it's a job that you have to grow with. Let us simply say that as a manager you will have a lot on your plate, and you have to enjoy being an ongoing student of human behavior to make the most of your work. Keep learning, all of the time, and you will do a great job.

Chapter 11

Owning It

It's just one step—one *giant* step—from being a manager to being an owner. Many of the same skills that distinguish good managers will apply to anyone who wants to own a restaurant. As an owner, you will need to motivate people, hire and fire, control costs, deal with crises . . . the whole nine managerial yards. On the other hand, being an owner comes with its own specific set of agonies and ecstasies. In this chapter, we open a window into the life of the restaurant owner, so you'll be able to get a good peek.

You will hear stories and advice that will inspire you, intimidate you, amuse you, and, hopefully, educate you. Even if you're not yet ready to move in the direction of ownership—even if you'll *never* be ready—you will no doubt find it interesting to hear what our panel of owners has to say.

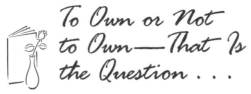

To Own or Not to Own—That Is the Question . . .

. . . and not a question to which we can give a definitive answer. But let's hear some thoughts on the topic from owners.

📖 Owning a restaurant is so different from working in a restaurant. It's like, suddenly, every night, you're giving a dinner party. And I'm not just talking about the food. It's the flowers. (*That florist slipped carnations in again!*) It's the glasses. (*Why are there streaks showing?*) It's the worrying about the spots on the carpet, and whether there's toilet paper in the bathroom. Did I mention the staff? Did I mention the issues of advertising and marketing? Did I mention what it was like to get a bad review from a food critic who wouldn't know a good meal if it came up and bit him in the . . . leg?

📖 Some people say that owning a restaurant is like having people into your home for dinner six nights a week, and there's some truth to that. But that's what I *like* about it. I've made my restaurant feel like an intimate home—or at least a heightened fantasy of what an intimate home should be like. I mean, let's get real—your mother never cooked the way I do. I mean, my mother never cooked the way I do! But you know what I mean. I've tried to infuse my place with a real sense of warmth and personal feeling, and my customers really appreciate it.

 The thing about owning a restaurant is that you're on task 24/7. Even if you're not physically *there*, you're there. You're always thinking about it. I take a two-week vacation in the summer, when I close the place down, and believe me, it's not like any two-week vacation I used to have when I was working for somebody else. Even when I was managing one of Houston's most popular restaurants, I still never worked as hard as I do owning my much-smaller operation in sleepy little Bucks County, Pennsylvania.

 I just *had* to own my own restaurant. I'd spent years working in places that were considered good, but when I thought about some of the substandard food they served, it killed me. Particularly for those prices! I just never felt right about what I did. Now, even though I'm struggling, I *do* feel right. There's a real pride and joy in giving people the best you can offer. And I'm not talking about the most expensive ingredients or the most awe-inspiring presentations. Just really good, honest food.

 You wouldn't believe my day. If I'm lucky, I get five hours of sleep. I come in at three in the morning. (Yeah—you read that right.) For five years, I was a manager of a top restaurant in Jacksonville, Florida, but my background—*way* back—was as a chef, and now that I own my own place, I'm cooking again. So there I am, in the middle of the night, setting set up my specials and writing out my orders with the place all to myself. Then, an hour later, my dishwasher comes in and starts cleaning. I take time to do a little yoga, which helps keep my head together. At 5 A.M., I'm placing the orders that I wrote out at 3 A.M. At 6 A.M, I start making my fancy cakes and tarts, which is one of the things we're known for (I actually started out in this business as a pastry chef). At noon, I cook lunch. At two, I take a break and catch up with people on the phone. At three, I'm back to work, meeting with the staff, going over reservations, and so on. At six, I'm cooking dinner. By 10, if I'm lucky, I'm out of there. Fortunately, I only live two blocks away. If I were any further, I don't think I'd make it home.

❝❞ You have to do it all, but you just *can't* do it all. You know what I mean? In other words, you have to be good at all the important things—managing, dealing with people, finances—but you shouldn't get into micromanaging. You need to give people some room, particularly your chefs.

❝❞ Not having to deal ultimately with any authority but your own is worth almost anything. Any aggravation, any disappointment, any frustration—it all pales before the pure joy of being your own boss.

Jumping In

How do you know when the time's right for making the big jump and starting your own restaurant? Let's hear how other professionals came to the decision.

🌀 I have to admit that I rushed into it. I was so intent on owning my own place that I didn't really give enough thought to how much learning was involved. I wish I had taken more business courses. You know, a lot of people who start restaurants have it in their blood. Their families are in the restaurant business, and they've been in the front of the house and the back of the house all their lives. I came to it pretty late in life, after a whole other career as a sales rep, and the learning curve was huge. And it's scary to have to learn on your feet when you've sunk a lot of your savings into what your gut is telling you could be a disaster.

🌀 Starting a restaurant is a little like having a baby. It changes your whole life. The amount of time and energy involved is unbelievable. Suddenly you have no time to spend with your partner, your kids, or your friends, and believe me, those relationships can suffer.

🌀 After a certain point, you need to make the leap . . . the leap of faith. If you keep telling yourself how much you don't know, then you'll never do it.

🌀 Network and talk to people as much as you can. And not just with restaurant owners, although you'll certainly want to do as much of that as you can. But you can also talk to other small business owners, your local business alliance, and so on. They can give you great tips on banking, insurance, and all sorts of things.

The How-To of Starting a Restaurant

We wouldn't dream of trying to tell you all you need to know about starting a restaurant in the small amount of space we have here. As in other places in this book, we just want to give you a "taste." Sweet? Salty? Sour? Bitter? The experience of opening a restaurant can draw on all of these flavors. Let's hear from the professionals.

If you really want to own a restaurant, the best thing is to totally learn the business from the ground up. Be a line cook. Work in the front of the house. Try purchasing. Become a manager. Before you own anything, you want to make sure you know everything you need to know about table service, the bar, credit cards, the whole bit.

Settling on your location can be a real challenge. I must have gone through 40 different "dream" locations before I found the one I finally settled on. At first, I was going to be in an office building. Then I was going to be near the big theater complex in town. Then I got freaked out about the rents, so I started looking in residential districts, at brownstones, maybe with a little garden in the back. But the code issues were hell, so I kept looking and thinking. I finally wound up down at the seaport, because I love seafood. Boy, did I luck out. This big seaport restoration came in after me, and suddenly my cheap, offbeat location couldn't have been more prime.

🌀 When you're picking out a location, you need to do what anybody who's looking for a store location would do. You sit in a parked car, like an FBI man, for days at a time, eating sandwiches, drinking coffee, and counting the passersby. If you don't see a lot of traffic, that means it's not worth the time, money, or effort to get started in that location.

🌀 Restaurant design is a big issue. If you're lucky, you're Wolfgang Puck, married to a top interior decorator like Barbara Lazaroff. Me, I'm lucky because I'm married to a wonderful woman, but she happens to be a nurse. So I started really small, with checkered tablecloths and hurricane lamps, but my food made up for it. Still, I find myself dreaming about skylights and zinc bars and all that stuff. Well, maybe one day . . .

🌀 I didn't have any real money for restaurant design, so I decided to make the whole focus be on an open kitchen. Well, that was the best decision I ever made. I even called my place "The Open Kitchen." People just sat there watching, like they were going to a show. And it's great for the kitchen staff too. They're putting on a performance every night, *and* they can't hide anything!

🌀 You can cut back on a lot of things when you design your restaurant. You don't need original art on the walls or customized paint jobs or wall-to-wall mirrors. What you can't stint on is good lighting. Lighting that makes the food look good and the customer look good is what it's all about. I guess by now you've figured out that I mean no fluorescents, right? Nothing makes food—or people—look worse than fluorescent light.

◖◗ I called upon an old friend, who is an extremely talented graphic artist, to pull together my graphic look—my logo and my menu, my matchbooks, my cards, all that stuff. It's so important. I think it's just as important as your restaurant design. Those things are your advertising. You're not going to be doing TV spots. A matchbook is the way you're going to get your name around, and mine was just stunning.

◖◗ It's just like starting any business. You need a whole marketing plan. You need to get stories about you placed in the papers; radio spots; you need to go on local TV and do demos. The whole nine yards. If you're not up for that, you may have a problem.

◖◗ Figure out your targeted customers before you open your doors. Are you in an affluent urban or suburban neighborhood? Better have some classic dishes that are handled "litely." That's what's selling these days. Leave fat out of your main courses, and put it into the desserts. People seem to want to eat "litely" and then have Death-by-Chocolate afterwards. Ah, zeze Americains!

◖◗ What really made my restaurant's reputation is that I became known for using a lot of local food growers, particularly those who raised crops organically. I wasn't strictly organic, but my interest in regional food growers struck a chord with the very liberal, educated clientele I was aiming for in my location. I'm in a college town, and people just really seemed to take to what I was trying to do.

✆ I found that a great place to make an impact is with your breadbasket. People are always dying to have good bread. They come in hungry, and it's the first thing they eat. And when you come down to it, what's better than bread anyway? Plus, for cheap and easy, you can make a big impression. I got into serving naan, the Indian breads, which are warm and puffy and perfect. People swoon over them. In fact, I think that some people come to my restaurant mostly for the naan.

✆ I introduced a cheese course at my place. The average diner hasn't had the experience of a cheese course after the main course, and it's really interesting and different for them, particularly when they sample the exquisite, perfectly ripened varieties. It brings a whole other dimension to dining and a whole other course you can charge for. It's been very popular and a great moneymaker.

✆ You'd better have great desserts, or you'll be very sorry. Most people in our society are crazed for desserts, especially when they go out to eat. You need a few real showstoppers. Pumpkin Cheesecake. Key Lime Soufflé. And, of course, something chocolatey and spectacular. Dessert is the last thing people eat, and it gets engraved on their memories.

✆ If you're opening a restaurant today, you've really got to invest, right from the start, in a good computer system. You'll be using computers to track inventory, make orders, handle reservations, do

Menu Planning

A checklist follows for plotting out your menu (of course, you can change a menu at any time, and when you do, go back to this checklist).

🐚 Is your menu set, or is it subject to change? Is the change seasonally driven?

🐚 What are your signature dishes? Do you have a showstopper?

🐚 Do you cook one basic cuisine, or do you borrow from many cuisines?

🐚 How large is your menu? Do you have the staff to cover a large menu?

🐚 What is the structure of your pricing? Do you offer items à la carte? Is yours a *prix fixe* system? Or is it *table d'hôte*, where you offer a single price for an entrée that includes something with it, such as vegetables or a salad?

🐚 How would you characterize the size of your portions?

🐚 Do you have a wine list?

🐚 Do you offer holiday meals?

🐚 Which meal of the day is your menu geared toward?

🐚 Is your menu descriptive, or do you rely on waitstaff to offer descriptions? If so, how are they trained for this?

your spreadsheets. Your system will act as a database for recipes; it'll help you create menus; it will track salaries; do your bookkeeping. Too bad it can't clarify butter!

💿 There are all kinds of competitive deals floating around when it comes to handling your credit card transactions. Check with your local business alliance or other owners.

💿 People starting businesses today are lucky, because they have such amazing technology available to them. We're six years into our restaurant now, and all of our reservations are done through a computerized reservations system. We've installed an on-line reservation system that uses advanced hand-written character recognition, sort of like a Palm Pilot™. That gives you a very low, nonintrusive profile at the front desk instead of one of those ugly big monitor things with a keyboard. The system gives you an instant "sketch" of any guest, so you know when they last dined with you, how many guests they brought with them, if it was a special occasion, and so on. Guests can also reserve over the Internet, which is great.

💿 Not all technology has to be expensive to be terrific. We have all of our front-of-the-house team wearing vibrating pagers now, which allows the kitchen to communicate with them. One buzz means that the food is arriving at your station; two buzzes means that the food is arriving at your partner's station; three buzzes means you're wanted in the kitchen to answer a question.

The People Part

The food and the ambiance are obviously important ingredients in a restaurant's success, but nothing will make or break your restaurant faster than service. Good service is memorable; bad service is unforgettable. You can be served an extremely delicious meal, but if you've been sitting in a restaurant virtually ignored for an hour, you won't even taste the deliciousness. And you will never come back. A critical part of an owner's job is to manage people, in conjunction with the manager, if you have one, and to ensure the best level of service possible. Let's hear some tips on this subject from professionals.

C Bad managing results in lost time. There are never enough hours in our day, and every minute is precious. So I think of people as a resource, and if I'm not dealing with them effectively, then I'm squandering that resource.

C Think "team." You're all in this together . . . or you should be. One way, obviously, to create a team spirit is to treat people fairly and to remunerate them fairly. Once you feel that you've been doing that, then you can focus on team-building activities, like sitting down all together to review the day and seeing how you can all maximize your time. The dishwasher, for instance, may be sitting around idle for a couple of hours. Couldn't he do a little prep work, which would not only utilize him more fully but might actually build his interest in his job, leading to a better chance of retention?

✴ Always try your very best to get your employees involved in your decision making. I'm talking about in both big and small ways. It makes them feel good, and you'll see how many good ideas will come of it.

✴ Educate your employees in what's involved in making money in a restaurant. At the very front of our employee manual, I have a picture of a dollar bill. Then I explain how much of that dollar bill goes to expenses—overhead, food, personnel, and so on. Your employees have to grasp the big picture, and then you can bring them in on the important stuff, like how they can sell and upgrade and stuff like that, to make more money for you and for them.

✴ I found a great way to make my waitstaff and bartenders happy. Instead of paying them their credit card tips every night, I put that money into their paychecks. So many of them blow the money when you give them dribs and drabs every night, but when they see this paycheck that's suddenly hugely inflated, they start doing things like putting down payments on cars or refrigerators. It's increased retention in my restaurant enormously.

✴ Always take the time to carefully explain a task. That's called "training." If you don't take the time, everybody will wind up losing time. Show the person where the right tools for the job are kept. Discuss what to do in case of a failure or an emergency. Teach them how to assess their own performance.

✆ It's crucial that you teach staff how to handle complaints promptly, courteously, and effectively. Not enough people get trained in handling complaints.

✆ Learn to communicate. Use easy-to-understand, concise language. Encourage questions. Ask if people understand you, and make sure that the climate you've created allows them to say no.

✆ Make sure that your work areas are clean, well stocked, well ventilated, and safe. The relationship of worker to task is always determined, to some extent, by the environment, and nowhere is that more the case than in a restaurant kitchen. Have regular staff meetings to bring to light any problems in that area.

✆ As the owner, you're not only the big cheese, but you're the role model . . . or at least you should be. Don't smoke, don't drink on the job, and don't eat excessively. Make sure your appearance is as immaculate as you want your staff's to be. Be ethical and honest—always.

✆ The more you relate personally to your staff, the more likely they are to relate to customers. And that's what it's all about. Nothing insures customer return like name recognition.

✆ Service in our restaurant is our #1 priority. It has to be. We already know we're great cooks. We treat every one of our customers like a visiting dignitary. A waitperson is at the table within 30 seconds of the customer being seated. Entrées all come out at the same time.

People feel pampered and loved, and they come back. No less than César Ritz said that "the customer is king." That was 80 years ago, and nothing has changed. The customer is still king.

🔊 A restaurant is no place for snobbism. A restaurant is where people spend their own money—and sometimes quite a lot of money—and they should be able to get what they want. If that means they want to drink Coke™ with their squab, so be it. It doesn't appeal to me, but it's not my business.

🔊 Some chefs will get very huffy about people coming in and going through a long list of dietary restrictions when they order. Some restaurants will even refuse to accommodate them, taking a "special orders *do* upset us" stance. In our restaurant, we look to accommodate people. We do no-salt, no-sugar, vegetarian dishes . . . whatever we have to do. After all, this is America in the twenty-first century. That's the way it is.

Quick Tips on Workers' Compensation

The cost of workers' compensation for small businesses is spiraling. How can you keep it in bounds? Some ideas from professionals follow:

🔊 Is your present plan being administered by a company that gives you quick results and turnover? If not, look elsewhere. It may cost them more

---

money to put more adjusters on the job, but if they don't do that, then it'll wind up costing *you* money.

🕮 You need to train your managers to report things promptly. The sooner you report a claim, the sooner the process begins of working with the employee to confirm the diagnosis, start the treatment, and hopefully get the individual back to work.

🕮 Restaurants are usually too small to have a Human Resources Department. We outsource to a team of registered nurses [that handles] the claims and the whole business.

🕮 Don't let an employee who has a problem just sit around collecting dust . . . or money. If he can't lift boxes, then maybe he can chop onions. Your comp management team can help figure out how to use this person safely and effectively. And alert your staff that in the event of certain injuries at least, this kind of transitional work will be the expectation.

🕮 I've noticed over the years that a lot of the claims brought against us are brought by wacky individuals who get wackier by the day, if not the hour, when they're home with their equally wacky spouses, parents, kids, or lovers. Keep them on the job somehow, instead of home in the asylum.

Promotion and Marketing

Another big concern for the restaurant owner is getting her or his establishment into the public eye and keeping it there. Owners comment on how it's done.

◖◗ I do a special meal once a week. It might be an Indonesian *rijstaffel,* it might be something Russian in the middle of the winter, like borscht and buckwheat blinis, or I might do a *tapas* event. I e-mail the menu to a large list of people, and that way they have an awareness of me at least once a week, even if I go into the trash with all the other spam . . . you should excuse the expression.

◖◗ I put together a newsletter several times a year that I send to my mailing list of customers and other friends and acquaintances. My wife and I both like to write, so we'll include reports of our trips to vineyards or other food sites, recipes, kitchen tips, and so forth. People seem to appreciate it.

◖◗ Wine tastings are a boon. They really get people into your restaurant in an easy way.

◖◗ Anyone who wants me on TV has got me. I don't care for what. If they ask, I show up.

◖◗ Obviously if you can hire a good PR person to help you with promotion, all the better. A PR person can help you form a strategy for a whole year or more—not just opening night. They'll orchestrate the practice dinners and the opening party. They may be able to snare journalists, celebrities, concierges from the big hotels, food world people—and all that matters.

✆ Establish an interactive Web site, and send your domain address to everyone you can think of. Post recipes, offer discounts, let your diners e-mail you with suggestions . . . you'll see how nicely it works.

✆ I often call customers after they've dined with us. "It was so nice to see you. How did you enjoy your meal?" Nobody minds, believe me. People like to think they're important enough that it's worth your time to call them.

Onward and Upward

Obviously there's a great deal more we could say regarding owning your own restaurant, but we're going to stop here. If you come to a place where you are seriously considering such a venture, you will have to spend months doing research, writing a business plan, learning about all of the statutes regarding work-ers' compensation and the laws regarding health regu-lations, educating yourself about taxes, and more. As we said at the top of this chapter, we just wanted to give you a "taste" here.

This whole book, in fact, has been designed to give you just a taste of the many different aspects of the restaurant profession. Continuing education is a must if you are to evolve and become the very best you can be. As an owner, you should constantly be seeking out the best restaurants and the best food. Visit and dine at the restaurants that win national awards, such as the Nation's Restaurant News Hall of Fame, and observe what is done that makes them unique. When you achieve what you set out to do, you will likely enjoy material comforts, community respect, the ongoing joy of doing what you do well for a living, and camaraderie with your colleagues. You have chosen a great field— never forget that.

Chapter 12

The Savvy Professional

It's time to take stock of where you are and where you are going. You work long, hard hours in a field that's very demanding. The good news is that you have the potential to make an excellent living. You're also in a field where there's a great deal of turnover. People have likened the restaurant business to a revolving door, and this has its pros and cons. The con is the frequent transitioning, which can be hard for some people, but the pro is the potential for quick advancement.

Generally speaking, success comes to those who work for it, and one way to do this is to manage your career smartly. You need to be flexible, *pro*active instead of *re*active, and always looking toward the future. If you're in a job that no longer feels right—let's say the standards of the kitchen are not up to snuff, or your employers do not know how to show their appreciation, or you're feeling burned out and that you're reached a dead end—then it's time to do something about it. Doing nothing is counter to success.

The good news is that the job market for restaurant professionals is picking up. After the downslide that followed September 11, the restaurant business is getting stronger, and more opportunities await you. Just make sure you go about your job search the right way.

For starters, the operative word for restaurant professionals wanting to explore the job market is "professional." You'll be graded on your attitude and attendance, which means you have to show up for work on time every day, and you have to prove that you know what it means to be a team player. If you develop a reputation for these traits, and if you know your way around a restaurant, then you should be in a good position when job hunting.

Laying the Groundwork

Even before you start looking for a job—and this is true whether it's your first, second, third, or fourteenth— always do a self-check of your current qualifications. Your colleagues recommend:

📖 If you're lucky, people will come after *you* for a job, instead of the other way around. You know, word of mouth is a big factor in the restaurant business, so this could happen. In most cases, however, you'll have to be the one that gets the ball rolling. Whenever I get into a job-hunting mode, I kick off the process by conducting a "review" of myself. I don't just sit there, waiting to find out how I'm seen by others. Instead, I "see" myself, even if I don't always like what I see.

🕮 Twice a year, whether I'm job hunting or not, I'll do a "report card" in which I "grade" myself. Is that weird? Maybe so, but it works for me. Here's what I do: I keep a checklist of attributes, and every six months I go through the list and assign a letter grade, A through F, for every one of these attributes. Punctuality? (I'm running a B there.) Teamwork? (B again.) Appearance? Efficiency? Speed? You get the idea, don't you?

🕮 It's important to have a solid self-image before you head out into the job market. Going for a job with shaky self-esteem is like climbing up a mountain with a 100-pound pack on your back. Ask close friends and any co-workers you can trust for feedback about your qualifications. Accept their constructive criticism. Act on it. If you feel you can't even go there, you might want to invest in a few sessions with a counselor to work on your self-image problems.

🕮 You really have to know what *you* want before you head out into the job market. Are you looking for security? The fast track? Flexible hours? More responsibility, or less? Where do you want to be in a year? Two years? Five years? Be clear about your passions and your priorities. It makes the job-hunting process so much more focused and easier.

Don't talk to me about "dream jobs." There's no such thing! Dream jobs are like dream families—do you know anyone who has one? Every job comes with its distinct set of problems, some worse than others. These problems are typically things like too much work, crazy people, long commutes, no room for advancement, or any and all of the above. It's up to you to figure out which of these problems you can or can't handle.

Calling It Quits

There's a right way and a wrong way to leave a job. Which will you choose?

My #1 piece of advice, which I'm sure you've heard from your mother, your father, your aunt, and your uncle, is never leave a job until you *have* a job. Even if you're miserably unhappy, try to tough it out, because you run the risk of being even less happy if you wind up being unemployed for an extended period of time.

You should be aware that you'll need to do some serious planning before you leave a job. For instance, there might be an area in which you need to brush up your skills. If you're going to an area of the country, for instance, where it would be extremely useful to be bilingual, you might want to take a Spanish course before you go after jobs there. Do some research, find out what you need, figure out what you don't have, and get it!

❰❰ Even if you've had a history of blowouts with your boss, it's a very good idea, when you finally leave for your new position, to make a nice, clean, friendly break. Don't say the things you always wanted to say. Write them down in a notebook instead, and stick the book in a drawer. If you're the one who has to be the bigger person, then just bite the bullet and do it. The fact is, if you leave with bad feelings, it can come back to haunt you.

❰❰ Never give less than two weeks' notice, no matter how bad things are. Your goal is to come across as a class act, no matter what, and bad habits, like leaving without sufficient notice, can become an unwanted part of your "résumé" that follows you around wherever you go. By the same token, never give more than four weeks' notice. Even if the situation is basically amicable, too much notice can leave you feeling quite strained and awkward.

❰❰ If you tell your employer that you're leaving, and he makes you a counter-offer, give it some serious thought. Why, in fact, are you leaving? If it's about the money, might it make more sense for you to stay than to transition into a new position? If it's about just wanting a change, do you think you might want to stay in the job if some changes were made?

❰❰ The best way for a person to leave a job is in the middle of a lovefest. Send personal thank-you notes to all the people you've worked with. Buy them presents. Take people out to lunch. It's so much nicer that way.

Regarding Résumés

The résumé is your most important tool when searching for a job. This written summary of your education and work experience will tell potential employers, at a glance, all about your achievements. Some thoughts from your colleagues on the subject of résumés follow:

 Keep it short and sweet. In a lot of fields, people are told that their résumés should not exceed one page in length. In the restaurant world, where there is so much turnover, it may be hard to do that. Still, you need to keep it compact. Don't go off on tangents about how you play the cornet in a Dixieland band. It's not relevant, unless maybe you're looking for a job in New Orleans.

 As a restaurant professional, surely you must realize that neatness counts. You wouldn't seat a diner at a table that had a mustard stain on the cloth or lipstick on the wineglasses. The same goes for your résumé. Make sure that everything is neat and clean, with no smudges or coffee stains or Lord knows what. Put your résumé on special quality résumé paper (this is a heavier stock that you can purchase in stationery stores). Don't go rainbow crazy. Maybe *you* think pink is your color, or that orange is cheerful, but other people might hate pink or orange, so why risk it? Stick with white, buff, or gray. To you, it might be boring, but to others, it's classic.

 You might have a great résumé in terms of layout and the accomplishments you're listing, but if you don't have the necessary contact information—address, phone number, e-mail address—then what good is it? Make sure that your contact information appears on your cover letter as well.

🕮 When it comes to résumés, there's a big argument over how best to arrange them. Check with a librarian or on the Internet for format. Some people like to arrange the résumé by listing their positions chronologically, while others like to arrange it according to their accomplishments or abilities. You'll have to check it out and decide for yourself.

🕮 Use simple language. Don't go overboard with all kinds of exaggerations. It just looks foolish.

🕮 Don't forget to list any honors and awards you've received.

🕮 Make sure your career goals pop out. If you're intent on working as a banquet sales manager, for instance, make that goal clear on your résumé.

🕮 If the line of work you're pursuing represents a career change, try to convey the transferable skills you'll be bringing with you to this new career. For instance, if you were a manager at a phone company in the past, pitch your managerial skills as part of your current package. After all, a big part of a restaurant professional's job usually involves managing people.

🕮 If you look at the literature on creating résumés, they'll stress how you should always use "action verbs." You *developed, achieved, created, coordinated, maintained, formulated, introduced*, and so on. These words make you sound like a powerful force . . . which you may very well be.

✆ Be extremely detail oriented, as scrupulous as you would be if you were taking a food order and didn't want to make any mistakes. On a résumé, misspellings and poor grammar can translate into points taken off. And in this competitive job market, you can't afford to lose points on stuff like that. Just ask a friend or family member to give your résumé the once-over. But make sure that person is a decent proofreader. (If necessary, go back to a professional résumé service, and draw on their resources for this task.)

✆ Nothing, nothing, nothing goes into the résumé about salary requirements. Could that be any clearer? Any talk about salary is restricted to your interview, and only if and when the interviewer brings the subject up.

✆ No photos please. They make a résumé look like the kind of "Most Wanted" notice you'd find in the post office.

✆ Don't bother including personal references on your résumé. It's safe to assume that everyone has someone who can speak well of him or her. Just list a few professional references. If a specific job asks for personal references on its job application, then that's another story.

✆ If nothing else, remember this rule: *never ever* lie on your résumé. If you do, and the grapevine gets hold of what you've done, you might have really serious problems finding a job in the town you live in.

Sample Résumé

A résumé that is well written follows. Of course, other kinds of formats also would be acceptable. Explore which one works best for you by consulting with a résumé writing service, your school, or knowledgeable individuals, or by looking for more information in career books or on-line. (The information that follows is from a real résumé but has been altered to protect the individual's privacy.)

Sharon McCoy

51-22 Bartholomew Avenue   435-889-0287
Wendell, Utah 12098
smccoy@hotmail.com

OBJECTIVE
Food & Beverage Manager

WORK EXPERIENCE

MARYLAND SOUTH FOOD SERVICES
Baltimore, Maryland
Dining Room Manager

- Responsible for entire service of 950-seat dining facility, supervising four assistant managers, 10 captains, and 60 waitstaff. Daily sales volume of over $250,000. Developed training system for new service procedures, as well as sanitation practices required by Maryland state law. Organized and trained staff in alcoholic beverage policies through TIPS program. Developed daily specials, in conjunction with the chef, which increased sales by 5 percent over previous year.

ROSEWELL FOOD SERVICES
CONCORD RACE COURSE—CAROUSEL RESTAURANT
Concord, New Hampshire
Sous Chef

- Responsible for expediting production of all food and minute-by-minute supervision of the staff for this 620-seat restaurant. Responsible for food sales of nearly $1 million in six weeks. Requested to work special functions, such as the Adams Gala Ball, serving fine dining to 350 people. One of four professionals chosen to work with two master chefs on special functions. Responsible for *creating daily specials* and preparing food for banquets held daily at the restaurants. Responsible for working as an expeditor and as a liaison between the front and back of the house. Gained a working knowledge of inventory and ordering procedures.

CAMERON'S ON THE LAKE
Harrington, New Hampshire
Line Cook

- Responsible for the production of all food for this 350-seat American-Italian restaurant. Started as a cold preparation cook and advanced to running "the line." Gained experience of high production for à la carte service of up to 1,200 people per day. Gained experience managing several preparations cooks and up to eight line cooks. Responsible for preparation of banquets of up to 250 people while continuing normal restaurant service.

FREEDOMVILLE REFRIGERATED LINES LTD.
Freedomville, New Hampshire
Operations/Dispatch

- Responsible for complete logistics of groceries for the entire Northeast for the 1.5 million square feet distribution center, including routing, tracking of shipments, and developing

detailed reports for management. Fleet included over
200 owner-operators, averaging 130 shipments per day.

Twelve years of front-of-the-house experience—Bartending in
lounge, nightclub, wedding and banquet venues.

EDUCATION

WASHINGTON COUNTY COMMUNITY COLLEGE
Washington, New Hampshire Associate in Occupational
Studies—Culinary Arts

- Completion date scheduled for May 2003
- ServSafe Sanitation Certification, 12/12/01 *TIPS (Training
  for Intervention Procedures), certified 03/20/02
- Recipient of the 2002 Lodge's Cooks Scholarship and the
  Marion Williams Scholarship
- Member of the American Culinary Federation (ACF)
- Member of Phi Theta Kappa—Alpha Upsilon Chapter

Cover Letters

Everybody talks about résumés, but the cover letter is just
as important. In fact, without a good one, a prospective
employer may never even get to a résumé. Professionals
explain what you need to know about this topic.

◖◗ The most important thing to keep in mind is that
your contact information has to be on your cover letter.
It's not enough just to have it on your résumé.

◖◗ If you're creative—as so many restaurant professionals are—then the cover letter is the place to put
some of that creativity, not your résumé. Develop an

interesting first sentence. Reference a quote. Do what you will to capture the attention of the person who may be reading your letter. But don't go overboard. Don't write a rap poem or draw a cartoon or whatever.

This may seem obvious, but you'd be surprised how many people just don't get it. *You never send a form letter for a job.* Every letter to every person must be completely customized.

Your letter should be personal and appealing, but brief. Don't go into any special circumstances. Don't tell them how you had to sell the family farm in order to go to school. Once you get your foot in the door—no, make that *beyond* the door—then you can get a little more personal.

Highlight your skills in your cover letter. If you've gotten special training of any sort, put it right up front in the cover letter. It's a way to grab attention.

Networking

Far and away, networking is the restaurant professional's best way to find a job. In the food world, as in most industries, the worst jobs are those that are advertised in the help wanted sections of newspapers. Relatively few job seekers obtain jobs through the "open" job market, which consists primarily of help wanted ads on the Internet or in print publications.

The food world is even more of a word-of-mouth industry than most, so networking is key. With your résumé in shape, you can start to target those people you think might be of help. Keep in mind, however, the following pointers from professionals:

◖◗ There's such a turnover in the food world that your best bet really is networking. I'm a restaurant manager, and I also teach at a community college, and I probably get three to five calls a week from people who are looking to fill openings on their staff. Some of the jobs are entry level; some are much higher up. If I know people who are looking for jobs, I'm happy to make the connections. That's the way it's done in this business.

◖◗ You want to know why networking works? Because it's based on real human nature. People aren't helping you because of the goodness of their hearts. People are helping you because they figure that down the line maybe you'll help them or their sons or daughters or nieces or nephews. And if you're smart, you will.

◖◗ Try volunteering with different organizations so you can get your name out there in the community of restaurant professionals. If you check into it, you'll probably find that there are fund-raisers scheduled in your area that you can help out at. These functions are a great way to get your foot in the door and make yourself noticed. If people see that you've got the right attitude, and that you know how to be a team player, they'll be happy to help you.

♨ You *never* stop networking. It's a state of mind. It's not like you reach a certain plateau in your career, and you just stop. You have to think of your career as a work in progress and networking as an ongoing activity that's positive and constructive.

♨ Once you start getting into a networking mode, even if you're relatively new to the food world, you'll start to see how many connections you can make already. There are friends, family members, faculty you've known, and all of their contacts, neighbors, merchants at stores where you shop regularly, people in your church or synagogue or other organizations in which you participate. Start keeping track of them, developing a Rolodex™ or a database, and you'll be surprised.

♨ Always carry an up-to-date business card. There is plenty of software on the market to help you make your own, or you can have a few hundred run off inexpensively at any of the big copy centers.

♨ Keep in mind that networking doesn't just happen at business functions. The whole point of networking is that there are all kinds of people out there who can help you. So if your cousin invites you to join her at her law firm's Christmas party, take your business card with you. Maybe you'll wind up talking to a partner whose spouse owns a restaurant. You never know . . .

♨ When you exchange cards with someone, take a second to jot down some bit of relevant information about that person on the back of his or her card.

Maybe the person was into sailing, as you are, or was an old movie buff. That kind of information will make for useful "openers" when you try to reconnect.

◖◗ Don't take it personally if someone doesn't seem interested in networking with you. It happens. Just move on.

◖◗ If someone helps you in the course of networking—whether it's an actual job lead or just some good information—show your appreciation. Drop the person an e-mail to say thanks. It makes a difference.

◖◗ Don't abuse these connections. If a person is open to networking with you, don't suddenly act like the two of you are the best of friends. That will turn off the other person very quickly.

◖◗ Next to public speaking, networking is the big fear for a lot of people. Mingling with strangers at cocktail parties used to be my idea of hell on earth. The way I got around it was by practicing with people outside of my work world. So I'd give myself an assignment. I'd go to my kids' Little League games, and I'd tell myself to strike up a conversation on the bleachers with someone I didn't know. Then I'd find other places where I could practice my skills. The more I did it, the better I got at it.

◖◗ Learning to mingle is a skill that, like any other skill, only gets better with practice. Don't get stuck with just one person at a networking event. That's not what it's for. Be friendly, and introduce yourself to as many people as you can.

🖋 Help others as much as you can. I'm of the belief that when you help other people, your good deeds come back to help you.

🖋 If you want to get a job, you've got to go after it. It's not going to come after you. I knew I wanted to work in food services at Disney World. It was just a dream I'd set for myself. So I went after anyone who was even close to Disney World. It took persistence, ingenuity, a tough hide, but within a year, I had my job. Of course, I had the qualifications too, which didn't hurt.

🖋 If you're still in school, take advantage of the guest speakers who come to lecture. Target them after their presentation—but nicely please—and ask if you could send them your résumé. Many will be open to such a proposition.

The All-Important Interview

The résumé and networking are designed to get your foot in the door. Now that you've done so, what's your next step? Your colleagues comment.

🖋 When you go for your interview, make sure, first and foremost, that you have identification with you. That means a Social Security number, a driver's license, the names and addresses of former employers, and the name and phone number of the nearest relative not living with you. Don't leave home without these!

📣 First impressions count for a lot. That's just the way the world works. Think of how you've felt on occasions when a blind date comes to your door. Well, when you go into an interview, you're the blind date. That means your grooming has to be impeccable. Clean, pressed clothes, polished shoes, clean fingernails . . . the whole bit.

📣 A lot of people these days really *hate* perfume, and probably nobody hates it more than people in the culinary field, who rightly believe that it interferes with smell and, ultimately, with taste. So forget about wearing perfume for your interview. In fact, kick the perfume habit altogether.

📣 Bring an extra copy of your résumé with you to the interview. Even though you may have sent one beforehand, it can't hurt to have another one with you.

📣 Smile. People like smiling faces.

📣 There's no being late for interviews . . . *ever!* You should figure that if you're just one minute late, or even 30 seconds, you've lost that job. Scout out the location of your interview a day in advance. Even if it's an hour away, make the run. It's worthwhile, because if you get lost on the day of your interview, even if you show up officially on time, you may still wind up looking all hassled and stressed, and that won't help anything.

📣 Whatever you do, do not criticize a former employer. It will only reflect poorly on you.

📣 Anticipate questions. Obviously you know that certain ones are going to be coming up. *Why do you want to work here? What do you think you could contribute to*

our operation? How would you handle a drunk customer?
You need to do your homework, and make sure that
you've got some good responses ready.

💿 I tell the people I mentor to compile as many possible interview questions as they think they might
encounter. Are you a team player? Are you flexible?
What are your career goals? Are there any obstacles
that would keep you from fulfilling your commit-
ments? What restaurants do you love? Any and all of
these may come up, so it helps to be prepared.

💿 Role-playing your interview with friends or family can be very useful. Just make sure you're doing it
with someone who knows how to take the charade
seriously.

💿 Hey, people—don't treat the interview like a coffee break, okay? You don't walk in with a cup of Java
or a can of Coke™ or some Ritz™ crackers . . . even if
this is the food world. You don't chew gum on an
interview. And smoking? Are we kidding?

💿 Sit up straight, and speak clearly, just like your
mother told you to.

💿 Don't rest your bag or any other items on the
interviewer's desk. Some people are very territorial,
and this will turn them off.

💿 There will come a critical point in the interview
when the interviewer will sit back and say, "Now do
you have any questions for me?" This is not a time to
sit there, looking pretty and shaking your head no. This

is a time for you to seem like an intelligent, engaged person. So come prepared with a few questions. Not a whole barrage of them—just a few well-chosen ones.

◖◉ Don't forget to follow up your interview with a thank-you note. It's required. And it will give you the opportunity to restate your eagerness to fill the position, which could wind up being a key factor if the interviewer is choosing between two or three people.

◖◉ Keep in mind that there are certain questions that an interviewer does not have the right to ask, and that you do not have to answer. Anything having to do with your race, religion, national origin or citizenship, age, marital status, sexual preference, disabilities, physical traits . . . these are all strictly off limits. If one of these questions comes up, you should politely but firmly state that you do not think the question is relevant to the position being filled, and that you would like to focus on those qualities and attributes that are relevant. The message should sink in, and your interviewer may actually wind up being impressed with your presence of mind.

Salary Negotiations

For some people, talking about money is like a trip to the dentist: they'll do anything to avoid it. But negotiating your salary is a natural part of the hiring process, so you must become comfortable with it so you can do it successfully. Some tips from professionals for negotiating salary include:

🌀 Do your homework. Know what the going rate is in the neighborhood for the position being filled. The more information you have, the more powerful your negotiating position will be.

🌀 Negotiating for a job is not like negotiating for a car. After you buy the car, you'll probably never see the seller again. But with job negotiations, if the hiring goes through, you'll be living with the person you've been negotiating with, so it's important to operate out of goodwill. Keep in mind that if you're being offered the position, that means that the employer you're negotiating with has made up his mind that you're the one for the job, and so you both have the same goal: to make this happen.

🌀 There are a lot of "extras" that factor into a total compensation package, and you need to be aware of what they are. It could be vacation time, health insurance, or whatever. Look into all of these, and weigh them carefully when you're making your deal.

🌀 Never lie. If you've got a job history, never say you made more on your last job than you actually did. On the other hand, you don't have to show all your cards. In a way, salary negotiations are a little like a game of poker . . . a bit of bluffing may come into play. Maybe your first time doing it, it won't go as well as you hoped. But with practice, you may wind up winning a few hands.

🕮 Bargaining is expected, but there comes a time when you run the risk of overkill. When you feel the offer is in the zone, then back off. Don't hold out for every last penny. Even if your demands are met, your employer may walk away from the experience feeling that he has hired a prima donna. Remember that negotiation is about give-and-take all around.

The restaurant world is filled with exciting possibilities at every level. Keep your eyes and ears open, be proactive about your career, continually educate yourself to develop more expertise, and go for it!

Index